The Light Railways of
Britain and Ireland

Rev Teddy Boston, on the footplate of Bagnall 0-4-0st *Pixie*. (*Anthony Burton*)

The Light Railways of
Britain and Ireland

Anthony Burton and
John Scott-Morgan

PEN & SWORD
TRANSPORT

Published in 2015 by
Pen & Sword Transport
an imprint of
Pen & Sword Books Ltd
47 Church Street
Barnsley
South Yorkshire
S70 2AS

ISBN 978 1 47382 706 6

A CIP catalogue record for this book is available from the British Library

Typeset by in Ehrhardt by
Mac Style Ltd, Bridlington, East Yorkshire

Printed and bound by Replika Press Pvt. Ltd.

Pen & Sword Books Ltd incorporates the imprints of Pen & Sword Archaeology, Atlas, Aviation,
Battleground, Discovery, Family History, History, Maritime, Military, Naval, Politics, Railways,
Select, Transport, True Crime, and Fiction, Frontline Books, Leo Cooper, Praetorian Press, Seaforth
Publishing and Wharncliffe.

For a complete list of Pen & Sword titles please contact
PEN & SWORD BOOKS LIMITED
47 Church Street, Barnsley, South Yorkshire, S70 2AS, England
E-mail: enquiries@pen-and-sword.co.uk
Website: www.pen-and-sword.co.uk

This book is dedicated to the memory of a good friend and light railway enthusiast, the Rev. Teddy Boston.

Contents

Preface

The aim of this book is to give a picture of the light railway age in Britain. The main text is principally concerned with the story of the railways and the running of the lines, with details of locomotives and rolling stock mainly given in the photographs and captions. The pictures are not intended simply as illustrations to the text, but tell their own parallel story of light railway development. The reader should not be surprised to find that an extensive treatment in words of a particular line will not be matched by a profusion of illustrations, nor that a line that is particularly well illustrated will not be given an equally full description in the text.

It has not been possible to give detailed histories of every single light railway in Britain, indeed since many had essentially similar stories it would have been tedious to do so. The authors have selected those descriptions and those illustrations which seem best to illustrate some important general point. Inevitably some readers will find that their own particular favourite has been omitted – we can only apologise and hope that what is included will compensate for what has been left out.

Finally, it always looks a little odd to see that two authors are credited with a book. Did they alternate sentences, or what? In this case, the main text is by Anthony Burton and the pictures were collected and captioned by John Scott Morgan.

Preface To The Second Edition

There have been substantial changes in the photographs: there are more than in the first edition, and approximately half of the illustrations that appear in this edition were not used in the previous version. The text for this edition has been updated, mainly to include changes in the surviving light railways.

Chapter One

A Railway Outing

Mention the name of York and what image comes to mind – the Minster, the Roman city, the Medieval streets or perhaps, if you happen to be a railway enthusiast, the splendid station, the no less magnificent railway hotel alongside and the National Railway Museum? All these are facets, in their way, of York the great city, York the tourist city. But there is also another aspect of the place. There is also a workaday York, a county town set amid rich agricultural land, a place with a living to earn. This was the York I came to in the summer of 1978, the city that had spread outside its old walls. It had an industrial face, yet looked outwards towards the fields and meadows of the Vale. This was Layerthorpe, home of the Derwent Valley Light Railway, in one sense the last of its kind.

Railways were not new to York when the little Derwent Valley line was born, for York was after all home to Hudson the Railway King himself. But these older railways were for those who steamed off to distant horizons; the Derwent Valley was built and run for local folk, and something of that intimate, home-grown atmosphere still clung to the line that bright day in 1978 as I hurried along to catch the afternoon train. The little tank engine, a J-72 class JOEM, stood muttering to itself in steamy whispers at the end of the platform like a cantankerous old man. It certainly looked aged for although it was only built in 1951, the class to which it belonged first saw light in the boiler back in 1898. The feeling of a cosy, comfortable old age was reinforced by the rolling stock, carriages decorated with tinted prints of landscapes by long – and justifiably – forgotten Royal Academicians. Every picture was, as befitted a local line, of Yorkshire scenes: Whitby and Robin Hood's Bay on one side, Bridlington and Scarborough on the other. They evoked memories of holiday excursions to the seaside, though this little line had never aspired to such glories. When complete it ran for just over 16 miles, but now it was down to the rump, for just 4½ miles were left. But although our train was to take us just over 4 miles along the line, it was to take us back in imagination over more than half a century in time.

We drew away smoothly through the industrial hinterland of York, though already there was a hint of the country straying into the town on the grass verges: willow herb, wild briar and thistle, a splash of poppy and a rich crop of blackberries. The latter were so plentiful that it might have been worth the company's while to resurrect one of the most attractive of the excursion trains that they ran in the 1920s – the 'Blackberry Specials'. This report appeared in the *Leeds Mercury* of 21 September 1928:

I travelled on a 'Blackberry Special' today. The passengers were carrying all kinds of bags, baskets and tins – and even buckets! Alighting at Skipwith, the party split into two sections. The station-master's wife led one party down the line, and the stationmaster himself directed the others to the best areas for blackberries.

Six hours later, when we returned to the station, every basket, tin – and bucket – was full.

Babies, 'flappers', and old people made up the happy crowd. One old lady of eighty declared it had been one of the most enjoyable outings of her life.

The station master, of course, is delighted with the resumption of passenger traffic. He directs passengers to the spots where blackberries are most plentiful; he acts as signalman, telegraphist, crossing keeper, and booking clerk, and warns visitors of the approaching danger of traffic on the common at the same time as he collects their tickets.

They used to run eight of these specials a year, each with as many as a thousand blackberry pickers. Our train would never have held that many, and one might find it harder these days to fill the baskets, for looking across the fields one could see the spaces left by uprooted hedgerows. But if those days have gone, then some things at least have not changed. As we passed the local primary school, the children rushed to wave at the train just as their grandparents would have done. Then we left the last of the town behind and it was out to the country and the flat fields. A level crossing with impatient motorists went by, with alongside it the simple crossing cottage, its walls smoke-blackened by a thousand passing trains. It was another level crossing that caused the company to erect the one and only signal on the line – more being unnecessary on a railway run on the one-engine-in-steam principle. Trains approaching this particular crossing from the direction of Elvington came up to it

round a sharp bend, giving the driver no time to stop should the gates have been left closed. The signal itself was connected to the gate, so that it was automatically pulled off when the gate was opened. Now even that one signal was superfluous, for trains no longer reached it.

The white plume drifted over the fields, the locomotive working steadily and rhythmically over the level way. There was a derisory whistle as it passed a scrap heap of rusting car chassis, most of them less than half the age of our engine. But the motorists got the last laugh as we came to halt at the buffers facing the busy main road. Dunnington station has no pretensions to grandeur; a simple structure of plasterboard on a wooden frame, not unlike an overgrown cricket pavilion. There was time to admire the engine as it ran round the train ready for the return journey. Time also to look over to the site of Dunnington Industrial Estate – land bought by the company in the hope of attracting new industry which would provide customers for the railway. And this was the factor that set the Derwent Valley Railway apart from all other preserved steam lines: it had never ceased to carry goods traffic since the day it first opened. Born in the early years of the century to carry freight and passengers, it still carried freight and passengers – the last of the line of light railways that had remained independent and at work. There had, however, been several major changes over the years.

The line had a modest beginning in a resolution carried unanimously by Riccall Rural District Council on 21 March 1898, proposing that they should build a railway. They also decided that the project might prove a little too ambitious for one rural council, so they called on neighbouring Escrick Council for support. The roll call of places to be served by the line gives a very clear notion of the sort of community it was to serve: Cliff Common, Skipwith, North Duffield, Thorganby, Cottingwith, Wheldrake, Sutton Newton, Kexby and Dunnington. These tiny rural communities were to be connected by rail to the main line between Selby and Market Weighton. It was to be a rural line serving rural needs, bringing passengers and produce to market. Indeed, within three years of opening, over seven thousand head of livestock were being carried annually.

But that is looking a little ahead of ourselves, for construction and the grand opening ceremony did not follow very quickly on the heels of that first meeting of the Rural District Council. It was not until 1910 that an order was placed with Patrick Dix of London for the actual building of the line – and it would not appear to have been the happiest of choices, for Messrs Patrick Dix and Company proved somewhat wayward in their financial dealings. Locals were regaled by a splendid new sporting pastime – 'Hunt the Loco', with the bailiffs trying to locate and impound the engine while the contractors tried, with surprising success, to hide it. None of this was, however, much help in getting the line completed, and it was something of a triumph when it was. In 1912 Lady Deramore cut the tape and the first train was on its way. Rather curiously, it ran out tender first, and as the tender was covered by flags and bunting the driver's view of the way ahead must have been decidedly limited.

So, at last, the railway was at work and passengers were provided with a fine new timetable, complete with a map of the route and descriptions of the delights on offer among the 'charming villages and natural beauties' of the Derwent valley and their 'comfortable inns with

modest charges' – just the thing it seemed for 'angler, nature lover, and picnic parties'. It was not, it might have added, just the thing for those in a tearing hurry. The timetable showed nine stops between Layerthorpe and Cliff Common, the junction with the North Eastern line, and a total journey time of 48 minutes for the 16 mile journey – 'subject to alterations' it added ominously. It was, in fact, common practice to run mixed trains of freight and passengers and it needs little imagination to conceive of the delays incurred by attaching and detaching goods waggons at the halts along the way.

When the railway began operation it owned a little rolling stock, mostly goods but including two coaches – but no locomotive. This was hired from the North Eastern Railway and served well until, in 1925, they bought a Sentinel geared locomotive, the first to be used in Britain. For a while all went well. In 1918 there were 564 first class passengers and 46,982 second class, but the 1920s and the days of the motor coach lay ahead. First class passengers dropped to 173 in 1924, to a mere 3 the following year, and none at all travelled in 1926. In the same period, the number of second class passengers fell from 23,171 to 5,381. The service ended, apart from a few excursion trains and specials. Freight traffic, however, continued to prosper, and although the peak loads of the early 1920s were never to be seen again loads remained at very respectable levels.

There followed two key events in the history of the line: nationalisation and the arrival of Beeching. Why, when it seemed that the whole railway system was to be nationalised, was the Derwent Valley left out of the scheme? In fact, it was by no means the only line to be so neglected; altogether twelve standard gauge and twelve narrow gauge lines, representing nearly 300 miles of railway were left out of the reckoning. Officialdom thought these lines to be insignificant. This was regarded as a mortal insult by the Yorkshire men who had worked like slaves to cope with massive demands during World War II, but there it was. The railway had begun as an independent concern, and as an independent concern it would continue. Then along came Dr Beeching. The Derwent Valley was not Beeching's concern, but the old Selby–Market Weighton line was – and was duly felled by his famous axe. Quite suddenly, the Derwent Valley had become a line that led to nowhere. It must have seemed that the end had been reached, and certainly the end of the original 1913 line had arrived. The axe had cut one line, and now the Derwent Valley had to be pruned as well, chopped back from 16 miles to just over 4. Fortunately, there were a number of small concerns that could still be served by rail, and a new bulk freight programme was begun.

There was one other lifeline that the railway could cling to – the growing enthusiasm for steam preservation. So, on that summer day I found the Derwent Valley still struggling on. Freight traffic for the previous year had run at nearly 50,000 tonnes and over 10,000 passengers had come along to ride the train. There was a decidedly chirpy air about the staff at Layerthorpe. Management talked with optimism about the future. The station staff talked irreverently about the 'ruddy slave drivers', but were still content to turn their hands to anything from ticket collecting to plate laying. The old tradition, it seemed, was lingering on. But before I left at the end of a very pleasant day, I was handed a copy of the company balance sheet for 1977, and the message printed there was being sung to a different tune. Read it how you would, one thing was clear: expenditure on the railway was running at £51,400 per annum, income stood at £46,722. It was not a message of hope. Over sixty years of light railway history were soon to come to an end. The last of the light railways, run as light railways were intended to be run, carrying both passengers and freight, was about to reach the end of the line. It was officially closed down and the last train to operate on the line ran on 27 September 1981. And that, everyone assumed was that, but the Derwent Valley had attracted the attention of enthusiasts who were determined to preserve something for the future. A Light Railway Order was issued for the section at Murton, which was a site that had an obvious advantage. It was also home to the Yorkshire Museum of Farming and it seemed reasonable to hope that visitors to the museum might like to pop across to the little station for a short line down the track and back again. Twelve years after it had closed, this section was up and running and steam locomotives again puffed down the line and they were able to celebrate the Derwent Valley's centenary.

Other preserved railways still run, some still running as they were when built, but these are special cases, such as the Romney, Hythe and Dymchurch. But the days of the commercial light railways were ended, and with their passing an era of British railway history ended as well. In this book we shall mourn their passing, but we shall be much more concerned with celebrating their achievements.

York Layerthorpe station, on the Derwent Valley Light Railway in the 1920s, with the Ford Rail Bus set waiting to depart with a local service. (*Photomatic*)

The Derwent Valley Light Railways 0-4-0 Sentinel locomotive, here seen shunting at York Layerthorpe station, c 1925. (*Photomatic*)

A wooden posted slotted signal on the Derwent Valley Light Railway, c 1925. (*Photomatic*)

Wheldrake station on the Derwent Valley Light Railway, c 1925. The buildings are of simple construction, with basic facilities and track layout. (*Photomatic*)

Chapter Two

Filling The Gaps

So far we have been blithely discussing light railways without making any attempt to define the term – a course of action for which there are good precedents. The government of the United Kingdom passed the Light Railway Act in 1896, and they, too, singularly failed to attempt even a vague definition. Authors, however, cannot claim the same latitude as governments, so here is a definition that must serve for this book at least. It is an adaption of a version first put forward by John Charles Mackay in his classic discourse on the subject first published in 1896 – providing, in fact, just that description that Parliament failed to provide that same year. A light railway is one constructed of lighter rails than those commonly in use on main lines, worked at a slower speed, providing poorer accommodation for passengers and less facilities for freight. It is a line that can be worked to less stringent standards of safety and signalling than apply elsewhere in the rail system. It should be, in short, a cheap railway. If this description makes the light railway sound very much like a second-class railway, then perhaps it is because that too is a reasonable working definition. The light railways *were* inferior to the great main line routes in terms of facilities offered and standards of operation. But – and the but is vital – without them whole communities would have been entirely deprived of the benefits of rail travel and rail freight. To paraphrase a popular advertisement of a few years ago: they reached the parts other railways failed to meet. Second rate they may have been in comparison with such giants as the Midland or the Great Western, but they never set themselves up to match their standards. Their aims were modest and, in a surprisingly large number of cases, they achieved those aims, and in doing so earned themselves the affection and respect of generations of rail users.

To understand the need for light railways you have to look back to the golden days of the Victorian era when the railway network first spread across the face of Britain. Then, it seemed, there was a fortune to be made by those who could push a railway across the country from, say, London to Birmingham or Newcastle to Edinburgh. There was also a very fair prospect of good profits for those who would join Peterborough to Leicester or Shrewsbury to Chester. But where was the profit in joining Tenterden to Bodiam? None, if you had to go to all the expense of obtaining an Act of Parliament to authorise construction, if you had to provide a track that could withstand the pounding of main line expresses, and signalling to cope with a rush of fast moving traffic. There was little prospect of gain if you needed to build impressive stations and staff them to the levels that were obtained on the major through routes. Yet the traffic was there. Inhabitants of villages wanted – and needed – to travel just as much as the residents of towns and cities. Farmers had as much need to move their stock of goods as did the mighty industrialists. It was simply that the needs of rural Britain were more modest than those of urban areas and could be met, to everyone's satisfaction, by a more modest railway system.

The notion that light railways had a part to play in the national network was well established by the latter part of the nineteenth century. The question that was not so easily decided was: what form should a light railway take? Realists had a simple practical answer. The nature of the railway should be determined by the nature of the work it had to do and the country through which it had to be built. Realists were, as always, outnumbered by partisans who were divided into opposing factions; those who felt that the answer lay with narrow gauge lines and those who argued for standard gauge, but built to less exacting specifications than those demanded for the main line. Each side could marshall powerful arguments. The standard gauge enthusiasts made great play of the evils of a break of gauge – the appalling costs of having to take goods out of one set of waggons on a little railway to place them in the larger waggons of a main line. Was it not, they demanded, just this break of gauge that bedevilled British railways for so long, with the rivalries between the adherents of Stephenson and Brunel? In reply to that, the narrow gauge men pointed out that trans-shipment was a normal part of railway operation. Did not the customer carry his goods to the station in a road waggon, store them in a warehouse and then transfer them to a railway truck? And did not the same goods again get moved from truck to warehouse to road at the other end of the line? With all those movements involved why should one more be

so bad? They then proceeded to point out the virtues of cheap construction that followed the use of a narrow gauge: the tighter bends the narrow system made possible meant that the engineers could hug the contours of the land more closely, reducing the need for expensive cuttings, embankments and viaducts. Back came the standard brigade. Civil engineering may be cheap, but what about mechanical engineering costs? Instead of being able to use existing equipment and rolling stock, everything would need to be specially manufactured. It was left to the more sensible men, such as Mackay, to point out the obvious – that the question of which gauge was more appropriate should be decided entirely on the basis of which suited the particular, circumstances of the route. In particular the nature of the terrain would often be a determining factor. He quoted statistics produced by the International Railway Congress for the costs of laying rails in different types of country. On level ground standard gauge was estimated as varying between £2,392 and £3,987 per mile, compared with £1,260 to £2,057 for 2ft 6in gauge. In very hilly country the comparative costs were £8,742 to £1,163 for standard gauge and £3,652 to £5,582 for narrow and by the time you reached a 'very mountainous' category, the differences were even more pronounced.

The lines that were built usually, but not always, opted for a solution dictated by common sense. Having said that, however, one is struck when looking over the whole of the light railway scene, more by its diversity than by any sense of coherence that it might possess. It is precisely this great diversity that makes light railways so fascinating, and we shall now look at a few of these routes in more detail, starting with the line which first brought steam locomotives to the narrow gauge.

The railway in question is the Festiniog (its Welshification by the addition of a second 'f to Ffestiniog is a modern phenomenon). The line was constructed to provide an outlet for the slate from Blaenau Ffestiniog, to bring it over the mountains to the sea so that it could be sent on its way to roof the houses of the growing industrial towns of England. A new port was to be developed, Porthmadog, named either after its chief promoter William Madocks or the legendary Prince Madog, who is said to have claimed America for the Welsh long before Columbus sailed the ocean blue. Either version is possible – which you consider the more probable depends on whether you are a romantic or a cynic. The joining of port and slate mines involved major civil engineering including the building of 'the cob', an embankment across the estuary. Porthmadog was intended to be more than just a new port, it was also meant to be a great cultural centre, which no doubt explains why the scheme received the enthusiastic backing of the poet Shelley. The cob was completed in 1811, but the Festiniog Railway Company was not formed until some twenty years later and began operations in 1836.

The line as built was constructed on the tramway principle of full trucks descending from quarries under gravity and empty trucks being hauled up by horses. The first engineer was James Spooner, but it was to be his son Charles Easton Spooner who was to take the line on into the steam age. This was no simple task, for the line rose 700ft in 12 miles with an average gradient of 1 in 92 and was also built to a very narrow gauge indeed, a mere 2ft.

In his own book on narrow gauge railways, published in 1879, Charles Spooner reproduced an eye witness account of the early experiments with steam locomotives in the 1860s, when two locomotives were in use, supplied by George England of the Hatcham Ironworks of New Cross, London. One engine, officially entitled *Little Giant*, was known unofficially as 'the boxer'; the pistons worked in a series of short arm jabs and the whole locomotive ducked and weaved quite dramatically as it made its way up the line. It was, it seems, an alarming experience to travel on the little engine, as a contemporary account makes clear: 'Over the old portions of the road a speed of 8 or 9 miles an hour is the greatest at which it is possible to run without incurring the risk of breaking the springs or loosening the driver's teeth.' Alarming though these early engines may have been, they worked sufficiently well for the Board of Trade to waive its old rules against passenger carrying on narrow gauge lines, and a new episode in railway history was begun. The early achievements were consolidated when George England and Company built the double-ended locomotives using the Fairlie design. These curious locomotives, which look for all the world as if two conventional locomotives have been backed into each other and stuck together, are in fact, articulated, double-bogied engines, with a four-wheel bogie set under each of the two boiler sections. These famous engines can still be seen on the Festiniog Railway today. It seemed to Spooner that these represented the final answer to all the problems of narrow gauge steam railways, but it soon became apparent that properly designed, conventional locomotives could be used for the task.

The Festiniog Railway suffered from having had its origins in the horse-drawn tramway era, for it had a very restricted loading gauge. The company wanted to make their coaches as big and comfortable as possible, with the result that in the narrow cuttings, passengers watched with awe as the carriage sides cleared the walls with literally only inches to spare. The railway needed to make the most of its new passenger traffic, for the slate trade began to decline in the early years of the twentieth century, mainly because the harbour at Porthmadog was unable to handle the larger vessels needed for the expanding trade. A new trade was sought, based neither on slate nor local passengers, but on holidaymakers. It was not seen at first as an essential part of the working railway, rather as a badly needed additional source of revenue – and as the century went on, so extra sources of revenue became more and more essential.

The recent history of the Festiniog Railway is that of many another light railway: declining freight traffic, and passenger traffic being increasingly diverted to motor coaches. To add to the problems on this particular line, the company decided to embark on a new grandiose scheme, just when economies were most needed. They became involved in the construction of the Welsh Highland Railway, which was intended to provide a narrow-gauge network joining Caernarvon to Beddgelert and Corwen to Porthmadog. Only a portion was ever built, but that portion proved expensive to construct and the hoped for revenue never materialised. It was a classic case of planners breaking the cardinal rule of light railway construction: never build a railway before you have established that a railway is needed. The Welsh Highland served a region with very little potential for freight and only a marginally better prospect for passengers. What little there was of the latter trade was to succumb with the arrival of the ubiquitous bus. The Festiniog Railway was saddled with an expensive appendage just when it needed all its resources for its own operations.

The decision may have been an unfortunate one as far as the original operators were concerned, but today's rail enthusiasts have reasons to be grateful. The Line between Caernarfon and Porthmadog has been reopened and offers the rare opportunity to travel behind one of a pair of 2-6-2+2-6-2 Beyer Garratts on a spectacular 25 mile journey through Snowdonia.

There was a brief period in the company's history when it came under the control of a gentleman who will feature largely on these pages, Colonel Holman Fred Stephens, but the Welsh did not take kindly to a manager who wanted to run the line from an office in Kent. Decline continued with the line teetering on the edge of disaster. It was pulled back from the brink when it was taken over by the Festiniog Railway Trust, now the majority shareholder in the Festiniog Railway Society Ltd which, as all rail enthusiasts know, runs the line. The excursion trade which was once such a tiny part of the enterprise is now the essential ingredient of success.

So, the Festiniog has run the full range of light railway possibilites, from a beginning outside the world of steam, through success to apparent irreversible decline and then on to glorious revival. It is fitting that the story should have a happy ending, for the Festiniog played a vital role as the first narrow gauge line to use steam traction and the first to be permitted to carry passengers. Other light railways developed from similar origins in the tramway era, but could not match the Festiniog story of continuing success, though one at least has an almost equal claim to fame, and helps to fill in another area of the light railway map.

The Swansea and Mumbles Railway – just one of many names applied to this line, but the one we shall stay with – was the fifth railway in

Britain to be sanctioned by Parliament. It was planned to run from the Swansea Canal to the stone quarries of Oystermouth, and the Act of 1804 specified that it was to be used for waggons and carriages pulled by men, horses or, rather significantly 'otherwise'. Why the otherwise? Some have suggested that it was no more than common prudence to keep all options open, in case some overprecise bureaucrat was to object to the use of, say, mules instead of horses. Others have pointed out that the Act was passed just after Trevithick's first successful experiments with a steam locomotive on the nearby Penydarren Tramway that ran from Merthyr Tydfil to Abercynon. Were the promoters already thinking in terms of the possible conversion of their conventional tramway into a steam railway? The official records, alas, leave all to speculation.

Nevertheless, the old tramway did have one important innovation to its credit that showed the way to future developments. On 25 March 1807 a local man, Benjamin French, agreed to pay the company £20 per annum for the privilege of running a passenger coach on the line. This would certainly seem to represent the very first occasion when a passenger service was run on a railway, even if the service consisted of nothing grander than a single carriage pulled by a single horse. Contemporary accounts tell us that there were two return trips, for which the passengers paid a single fare of one shilling, but these early accounts differ very greatly in their views of what passengers got for their money. The Georgian traveller was both a hardy and an inquisitive soul, as interested in the latest on the industrial scene as in romantic ruins and picturesque landscapes, and travellers of both sexes expounded on all subjects with equal enthusiasm. Surprisingly perhaps, since our

view of the female of the age tends to be one of a delicate little flower that might wilt if exposed to anything as vulgar as the open air, it is the lady traveller who best survived the rigours of travel on the Swansea and Mumbles Railway. Miss Spence described how, in 1808, she went on a trip down the line and 'never spent an afternoon with more delight' than in the journey to Oystermouth.

Richard Ayton, author of one of the classic travel books of the period *A Voyage round Great Britain in the Year 1815*, was somewhat less enthusiastic. He described the sixteen-seat carriage built of iron and carried on iron wheels on the iron rails. It trundled along at little better than a brisk walking pace to the accompaniment of the noise of twenty sledge hammers in full play. The short rails mounted on stone sleeper blocks were not, it seems, conducive to a smooth ride. The poor passenger, hurled around the carriage, emerged 'in a state of dizziness and confusion of the sense that it is well if he recovers from in a week', Ayton wrote. Miss Spence was clearly made of sterner stuff than Mr Ayton, but one cannot help feeling that the latter's description must have been a fairly accurate one of travelling in an unsprung, iron coach over short irregular iron rails.

Over the next few years, the fortunes of the railway fluctuated considerably though, on balance, there seemed to be a great many more downs than ups. A major change arrived with the formation of the Swansea Improvements and Tramways Company in 1874, who were to build a system of horse tramways in Swansea itself, but who were also empowered to use the older line out to Oystermouth. So two different tramway concepts came together; the earlier idea of a tramway as a railway for carrying goods and the more familiar notion of a street tramway for the carriage of passengers. At first the street tramways were forbidden by the Act of Parliament from operating with anything other than animal power, unless they obtained a special dispensation. Other countries had powered tramways, but Britain was unable to join in the movement until the 1870s.

The new Swansea tramway was among the first to make the transition from horses to steam. Henry Hughes of Loughborough designed a locomotive intended specifically for tramways, which was very quiet and neither blew out steam nor smoke, for the steam was condensed and reused as feed water for the boiler and the locomotive was designed to run on smokeless coke. The engine was given successful trials in Leicester and then brought down for use on the Swansea line. Not every local dignitary was convinced of the benefits of steam railways being run beside busy roads, in spite of Hughes' assurance about the tranquillity of his engine. The Mayor of Swansea opposed the notion. He turned up on his horse, but after bringing the animal's head right up to the steaming engine without the beast showing even the slightest interest in the machine, he was forced to admit that whatever else a steam tramway might do it did not frighten the horses.

The problems of the line were not yet over, for although the tramway company had established rights to run over the railway, the old line was still in trouble. It was sold and arguments between the new owners and the tramway company soon developed, eventually to be settled in court with a bizarre compromise. The court ruled that the tramway company could follow each conventional steam train with a horse-drawn tram. So the line was run again as a conventional railway with conventional steam locomotives, but shared its services with the horse-drawn trams. More changes were to follow, with more changes of ownership, realignment and an extension to a new pier at Mumbles Head. This brought fresh traffic to the route and it emerged as a popular holiday attraction. Bank holidays saw as many as 40,000 passengers being carried on the little line, and the importance of the holiday trade by now far outstripped that of goods traffic. A final stage was reached with electrification of the line in 1929. It lost the look of a railway and took on the appearance of a seaside tramway. It finally closed in 1960, after more than a century and a half of use which had seen horse traction, steam traction and finally electric traction. There may have been more important railways than the Swansea and Mumbles, but few that could boast a more varied history.

The steam tramway had an important role in the early development of light railways. A pioneer – and one much more typical of the light railway movement – was the Wantage tramway. The town of Wantage in Berkshire was, and is, a pleasant country town surrounded by rich agricultural land. It also had a further claim to fame in the Wantage Engineering Company, founded in 1847, which was to become an important manufacturer of traction engines and steam waggons. None of this, however, proved sufficient an attraction to persuade the moguls of the Great Western Railway to bring their lines to the town itself. The best they were prepared to offer was Wantage Road Station on the main line from Swindon to Paddington, but a full 2½ miles from the town. A horse bus provided an infrequent, inadequate and expensive service. These were precisely the circumstances that were suited to some form of light railway, as a local ditty made clear:

From the station to Wantage an omnibus runs –
A small one – now pray do not laugh,
When I tell you the fare they charge over there
Is a 'bob'[1] for two miles and a half …

They think bye and bye the rail will be nigh,
And then at the bus they will laugh;
They will ride in good style at a penny a mile
and no 'bobs' for two miles and a half.

The local citizens banded together to promote a horse tramway which was opened in 1875. It was a single line running alongside the main Wantage to Oxford Road. It connected the GWR main line to the town, with a couple of halts along the way, a goods depot and a short branch to serve the gas works. It was not destined to remain a horse tramway for very long. In 1872 John Grantham designed a composite steam tramcar. It was 30ft long, mounted on two pairs of wheels, only one pair of which were drive wheels. The engine was in the centre of the car and there was room for twenty passengers inside and twenty-four passengers outside. The first trials were held in London, when it performed quite successfully on the tramway between Victoria and Vauxhall Bridge. When a similar car was built for the Wantage line, however, it failed to cope with the steep 1 in 47 gradient, and so it was given a new Merryweather boiler and the length was reduced to 27ft 3ins to ease the way round the sharp tramway curves. In its new form the engine worked quite satisfactorily and was soon joined by a locomotive built by Merryweather of London, who specialised in tramway engines. There was a brief flirtation with a compressed air engine, about which not

a great deal is known, but as it was the one and only engine of this type used on the line one can assume it was not a great success.

Steam soon returned and remained on the line right through until closure, the little engines chugging along beside the main road for well over half a century. Passenger services, however, were withdrawn in 1925 and by the end of the Second World War goods traffic too had come to a halt. In 1946 the line was closed. The Wantage tramway had been one of the first roadside steam tramways in Britain – and it also proved to be the last. It was a line with no delusions of grandeur. It had a simple job to do and it did it well, typifying the virtues of so many similar lines. Its very longevity is a measure of its worth and its success helped to stimulate interest in the whole idea of light railways. It was only one of many tramways which took a variety of forms, from the mineral railways such as the Glyn Valley Tramway which, like the Swansea and Mumbles line, was an adaptation of an older horse-worked line to the Wisbech and Upwell Tramway, serving the agricultural interests of East Anglia. They all went a long way towards proving that the light railway had a considerable role to play in serving the needs of small communities throughout Britain. Many engineers and businessmen accepted the theory, but still felt that there were too many obstacles to overcome before the light railway dream – every community with its own rail access – could be realised.

The difficulties facing would-be railway constructors were inextricably tied up in the complex of railway legislation. At the very start, before work could even begin, there was all the trauma and expense of obtaining an Act of Parliament. Assuming an Act was obtained authorising the line, this merely

---

1. Younger readers will need to know that a 'bob' was a shilling, 12 pence In old coinage, 5p today, the equivalent of £3.50 at today's prices.

opened the door to new problems – land had to be bought, complex regulations obeyed regarding safety, signalling and the like. The trouble was that no distinction was made in law between the least significant branch line and the mightiest trunk route. Various pieces of legislation were enacted to ease the way for potential light railway promoters, notably the Regulation of Railway Act of 1868, which had a section specifically relating to light railways, and the Tramways Act of 1870, though the latter was very much tuned to the needs of urban tramways. Life was still not easy for light railway builders, and that meant that costs were frequently too high to offer much hope of profit for those prepared to fight their way through the legal tangles.

The difficulties faced by companies wishing to promote short routes to meet local needs could scarcely be better exemplified than in the case of the Easingwold Railway. The aim of the planners was simple: to link the small Yorkshire town to the North Eastern Railway at Alne, a mere 2½ miles away. What could be simpler? But before the line could be begun, a special Act of Parliament had to be obtained which decreed that the railway must be built to the exacting standards of a main line. In spite of all the difficulties, the line was built but it took from 1887 to 1891 to complete it and it cost £17,000. Compare this with the Corringham Light Railway just a quarter of a mile longer, built across the Essex marshes near Tilbury. Opened in 1901, less than two years after it first appeared as a gleam in the planner's eye, it cost only half as much as the Easingwold. What was the difference? What had happened in the period between the building of the two lines? The answer is the passing of the Light Railways Act of 1896.

The Act was a masterpiece of vagueness, with not even the concept of a light railway being considered as needing definition. Many people at the time thought this to be a distinct advantage, giving maximum freedom to railway builders who could define the term to suit their own needs. What seems not to have been noticed was that the new Act left the rules set by earlier Acts unchanged, so that for example maximum speed limits were still set at 25mph. Whatever its shortcomings the Act did have one great virtue – it cut away whole skeins of red tape. Instead of having to apply for a special Act of Parliament, the promoters need only apply to the newly formed three-man Light Railway Commission for a Light Railway Order. Other troublesome matters, such as land purchase, were also greatly simplified. It was now possible to build railways which would never have been financially viable in the days before the Act. Some of the provisions of the Act looked particularly fine on paper but were to prove less useful in practice, particularly those designed to encourage local authorities to become actively involved in railway construction. The objectives of the Act were clear and admirable – to enable local communities to build and run their own railways. Not all who took advantage of the new law had quite the same end in view. In the first twenty-five years after the passing of the Act some 700 applications for orders were made. Some were impractical to the point of frivolity, some orders were granted but nothing was ever seen on the ground and of the minority that were built, not all were constructed from the high motives assumed by those who framed the law.

The Basingstoke and Alton Railway was a case in point. It was promoted by the London and South Western Railway not because they particularly wanted a line from Basingstoke to Alton, but because the Great Western Railway had designs on coming through the area to grab a share of the lucrative Portsmouth traffic. The LSWR reasoned that if they could get a light railway down on the ground then it would effectively block their rival's plans. The price of construction proved to be a mere £67,000 for the entire run of 13 miles, a small price to pay for retaining their local monopoly. And there was even a remote possibility that the new line might show a profit, though there is little evidence of this view being widely held among the board of directors. The line left the LSWR main line near Basingstoke en route for Alton, along the way contriving to miss all the intervening villages. The luckiest citizens were those of Cliddesdon who had a station a mere half mile from the village, but they only got that because the parish council made a fuss. The company had wanted to put their lines further out to keep to a perfect level and reluctantly agreed to the move which involved them in having to put up with a 1 in 330 gradient. A reporter from the local paper, the *Hampshire Herald* and *Alton Gazette*, travelled on the first train in June 1901 and was not unduly impressed. It was an unspectacular opening: no fireworks, no bands, no fanfares – not even any dignitaries. It was inaugurated, as he wrily remarked, 'with a modesty thoroughly in keeping with the provision for the requirements of the public which the new line will afford'. There were only three trains a day and there was no danger of breaking the provisions of the Act since the average speed was a mere 13mph, though at various points along the route where the curves became unusually sinuous, boards were set informing drivers to keep below 10mph. The railway provided rough corrugated iron sheds as stations, but at least did not stint on staff provision, for each station was dignified by the presence of a stationmaster who was not, one may assume, over extended by his duties.

It is no surprise to turn up the records of this lackadaisical line and find that it failed to show a profit, so that passenger services were withdrawn in 1932 with as little fuss and ceremony as they had begun. The end of goods traffic followed soon after. This was not quite the end for the old railway. It enjoyed a moment of glory on the silver screen when, in 1928, it had been used for a spectacular rail crash that appeared in the film The *Wrecker*. But true immortality came after closure when the little station of Cliddesdon was transformed into Buggleskelly on the mythical Southern Railway of Northern Ireland. The film which occasioned the transformation was that classic of British cinema comedy, *Oh, Mr Porter!* which starred Will Hay as the stationmaster, matched for incompetence by his staff of Moore Marriott and Graham Moffatt. Many a film has been made with a railway setting but never one which displayed such sympathy for the old railways, and none has ever bred such affection among railway enthusiasts. It was a film deeply imbued with light railway history, for it was not just the station that had been found on the light railway scene. The locomotive that had a starring role, *Gladstone*, as it was named in the film, had served on the West Clevedon and Portishead line, had been transferred to the East Kent Railway and, after its short appearance in the limelight, was sent to end its days as No 2 Northiam on the Kent and East Sussex Railway. It is a film of which this viewer at least never tires and one sequence in particular seems to sum up the quirkiness and unrealiability of some of the old lines. Will Hay arrives at

Buggleskelly and raps at the booking office window. The shutter shoots up to reveal Moore Marriott who announces firmly 'next train's gone' before slamming the shutter down again. Life on the old Basingstoke and Alton Railway may have provided a better service than that, but not much better.

The Basingstoke and Alton Railway failed largely because no one was unduly concerned to make it a success. Once the line was built it had already achieved its principal objective of blocking the advance of the GWR into Hampshire. But even before the passing of the Light Railway Act, lines had been constructed which even the most rosy-spectacled optimist could never have considered as anything but losers. The Bishop's Castle Railway is a classic example. It set off in 1861 with the best intentions, to join the Shrewsbury to Hereford line at Craven Arms to the Oswestry and Newtown Railway at Montgomery. It never achieved the aims set out by the promoters, but only struggled along to the half-way mark at Bishop's Castle. There was little industry along the way, few people – nothing in fact to provide a revenue. The line achieved the notable, if unwelcome, distinction of only breaking even in one year throughout its entire working life. It does, however, qualify for an odd little footnote to railway history in that it maintained the tradition of the Parliamentary Fare by providing one train every day on which passengers could travel at the rate of 1 penny per mile. This had been a condition imposed on the early lines by Parliament, but only the Bishop's Castle stayed

with it to the bitter end. That end arrived in 1935. No doubt the directors felt that as they were losing money on all their other operations, one more loss maker, especially one hallowed by tradition and Her Majesty's Government, could make little difference.

The major handicap under which the Bishop's Castle Railway laboured was that of working a line for which no discernible traffic existed. Many light railways attempted to follow their lead and although many concerns foundered before a single rail was spiked, some at least managed to pursue them all the way down the road to penury. There were lines such as the Leek and Manifold which we shall be looking at in more detail later, which appeared to run from nowhere in particular to somewhere very similar. The sad part about such stories is that very often – and the Leek and Manifold is an excellent example – such lines were built to the very highest engineering standards. It would be quite wrong, however, to suppose that all light railways were, by their very nature, doomed to failure. Many a line succeeded in ably fulfilling the function it was built to serve and if such lines seldom made spectacular profits, neither did they make the sensational losses of some of their compatriots. Success depended on good initial planning based on an accurate estimate of likely traffic, and efficient management once the line was completed. To see what this meant in practice we shall now look at a typical light railway in rather more detail, the Rother Valley Railway, later to be known as the Kent and East Sussex Railway.

A test train at Creuau in 1872, on the Festiniog Railway with the first Double Fairlie 0-4 4-0 tank locomotive, *Little Wonder*, hauling a long test train of freight wagons and four-wheeled carriage stock. The Festiniog Railway was noted as one of the first railways in the world to successfully use articulated locomotives of the type designed by Robert Fairlie. (*Author's Collection*)

An early photograph of the Festiniog Railway, c 1870s, taken at Tan-y-Bwlch station, showing passenger and mixed trains about to pass each other. The locomotive facing the camera is a single Fairlie articulated 0-4-4 tank, which along with the Double Fairlie type locomotives operated on the line at this time. (*Author's Collection*)

A Festiniog 0-4 4-0 double Fairlie Locomotive blasts its way uphill near Tan-y-Bwlch, c 1935. (*L C G B Ken Nunn Collection*)

Festiniog, England constructed 0-4-0 tender tank locomotive *Palmerston* with a train at Portmadog harbour station, c 1935. (*Local postcard*)

Festiniog Railway
disc signal, c 1910.
(*Author's Collection*)

The North Wales Narrow Gauge Railway was also a user of single Fairlie articulated locomotives. Here we see 0-6-4 tank *Moel Triyfan* with a train of mixed bogie and articulated cleminson carriage stock, c 1900. (*Author's Collection*)

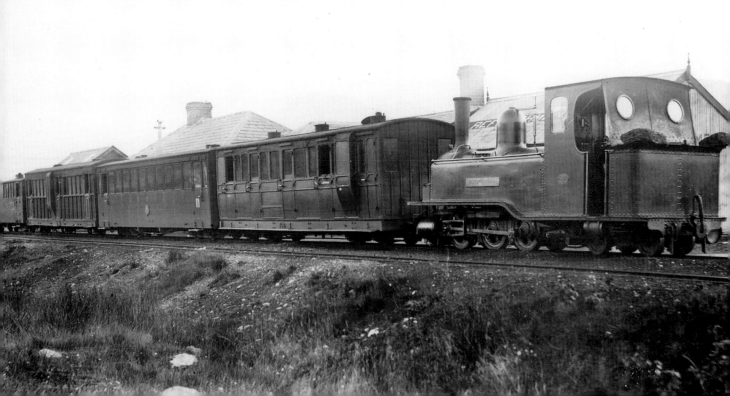

Fairlie articulated 0-6-4 tank *Snowden Ranger* stands in Dinas Junction with a passenger train for Rhydd Ddu, c 1905. The North Wales Narrow Gauge Railway closed to all traffic on 31 October 1916, being revived as the Welsh Highland Railway by Colonel Stephens, and extended to Portmadoc as part of his empire of light railways in 1923. The line closed again to passenger traffic in 1936 and freight in 1937, after which it was dismantled in 1941. During the 1990s the whole line was restored and is now a thriving heritage railway, carrying thousands of passengers each year through the Snowdonia National Park. (*Author's collection*)

Hunslet 2-6-2 tank, *Russell*, on a Welsh Highland Railway train at Beddgelert station on 8 August 1935. This locomotive was modified to fit through Moeyn tunnel on the Festiniog Railway, in order to allow through running to both lines. (*H. F. Wheeler*)

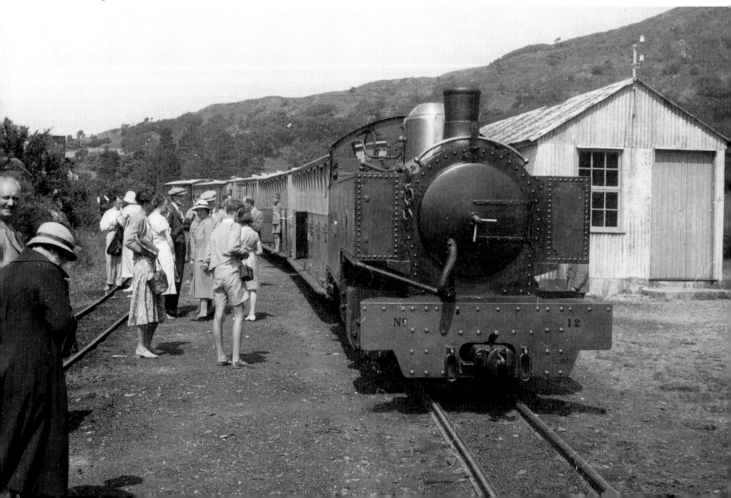

Mumbles Tramway, *Hawthorn Leslie* 0-4-0st and train of double and single deck tram cars, c 1900. The line was one of Britain's earliest tramways opened as the Oystermouth railway in 1806, later replaced by a parallel steam tramway in 1893, which in turn was electrified in 1929. The Swansea and Mumbles tramway was later owned by South Wales Transport, who closed the line on 5 January 1963. (*Author's Collection*)

A long train of double deck tramcars at Mumbles pier after decanting its heavy load of passengers, c 1910. The extension line to Mumbles Pier closed to traffic on 11 October 1959, three years before the rest of the line. (*Author's Collection*)

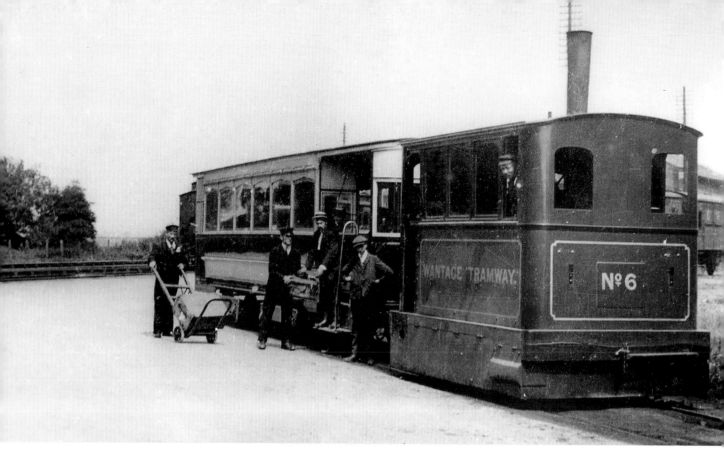

Fox Walker constructed 0-4-0 tram engine number 6 stands with a service for Wantage Town at Wantage Road station, c 1920. The Wantage Tramway was opened on 11 October 1875, providing a tram link between Wantage Road station on the Great Western main line to Bristol, South Wales and Wantage Town. The line closed to passengers on 1 August 1925 and to freight in May 1946. (*Local Post Card*)

Manning Wardle 0-4-0ST number 7 with the bogie tram car at Grove, c 1925. This picture shows the rural nature of this roadside tramway in the last decade of passenger operation. (*Local Postcard*)

Wantage Tramway number 5, with a train of bogie and four wheeler tram cars near Oxford Lane Halt, in the early 1920s. Locomotive number 5 was constructed by George England in 1857 and originally named *Shannon*, for the Sandy & Potton Railway in Bedfordshire, later becoming an L N W R locomotive, before being purchased for the Wantage Tramway where it was known as number 5, *Jane*. Number 5 is now preserved at Didcot Railway Centre and is owned by the National Collection. (*Authors Collection*)

A line up of three Wantage Tramway Locomotives. From right to left, Fox Walker number 6, Manning Wardle number 7, Mary and George England number 5, *Jane*, seen in the yard at Wantage, c 1910. (*Local Post Card*)

Hudswell Clarke constructed 0-6-0st Easingwold Railway number 2, simmers in the platform at Alne, with a mixed train of one four-wheeler carriage and some wagons for Easingwold, c 1925. The Easingwold railway was one of the first light railways in Britain, opening in 1891 from Alne on the North Eastern main line, to Easingwold, a distance of 2½ miles. The railway only had two locomotives in its whole existence, both were Hudswell Clarke 0-6-0st, number 1, *Easingwold*, constructed in 1891, and an almost identical replacement number 2 constructed in 1903. (*Author's Collection*)

Easingwold Railway number 2, in the yard at Easingwold, posing for a photograph with the staff and local children, c 1910. The original ex-North Eastern four wheeled carriages were later replaced with two ex-North London teak bodied four wheelers, seen here. This is a jolly period scene, with what appears to be all the local railway staff and the general manager, in suit and boater, not forgetting the dog on the footplate of number 2. (*Local Post Card*)

A general view of Easingwold station and its approach road, showing the rather basic station building, with a train just arriving, c 1900. (*Author's Collection*)

The Basingstoke and Alton light railway was constructed by the London & South Western Railway, as a blocking line to prevent the Great Western from going south from Basingstoke. Opened on 1 June 1901 and running south from Basingstoke via Cliddesden, Harriard and Bentworth, over 14½ miles to Alton. The stations were basic to say the least, this being Cliddesden, where the Will Hay film *Oh Mr Porter* was filmed in the 1930s. A second film was made on this line in the 1930s, *The Wrecker*, when a withdrawn ex-S E C R, F 1, 4-4-0 and a rake of birdcage stock were deliberately crashed into a steam wagon on a level crossing to add thrills to a film. The line was not a financial success and was closed and lifted in the First World War, however due to public pressure the Southern Railway was forced to relay the whole line in 1924, only to close it again to passengers on 12 September 1932 and to freight on 1 June 1936. (*Author's Collection*)

The Bishops Castle Railway was a light railway by default, in that it was part of a main cross country line from Craven Arms to Montgomery. Opened on 1 February 1866, only the first part of the railway was ever constructed, from Craven Arms to Bishops Castle via Lydham Heath. As a result of the collapse of Overand Gurneys Bank in London, who had overstretched themselves with railway investments, the company could not extend to Montgomery and quickly found itself bankrupt. The company found itself in the hands of a receiver from 1866 until its closure on 20 April 1935. Locomotive number 1, ex-Great Western number 567, a Dean 0-4-2 tank purchased in 1905, brings its ramshackle train of ex-Hull and Barnsley and L S W R carriage stock in to Craven Arms station, c 1930. (*W. Potter*)

Smoke drifts from the chimney of a sleepy Horderley station in this 1932 photograph, less than three years from the Bishops Castle Railways closure. The overgrown nature of the track work, with its 1860s period signals and its time worn buildings, needing a coat of paint, give the station an almost 'Will Hay' look. In the immortal words of the Buggelskelly booking clerk 'the next trains gone'. (*Author's Collection*)

Probably one of the most attractive light railway locomotives of all time, *Carlisle*, a Kitson constructed contractors 0-6-0 tender goods of 1868, purchased by the Bishops Castle Railway in 1895. *Carlisle* was the last Bishops Castle locomotive in steam used to demolish the line and lift the track after closure in 1935. Here seen at Bishops Castle on 30 May 1932. (*H. C. Casserley*)

Former Hull and Barnsley four-wheel carriage at Bishops Castle station on 30 May 1932, showing its second and third class designation, displayed on its doors. The Bishops Castle Railway had three classes of travel right up to its closure in 1935, that of first, second and third. (*H. C. Casserley*)

Chapter Three

The Railway At Work

The great names of railway history are invariably, and inevitably, those of the engineers – the men who built the first lines; Stephenson, father and son, Brunel or the builders of famous locomotives Gooch, Gresley, Ivatt, Stirling and so many more. A very few achieved infamy, the railway king Hudson having pride of place in this particular rogues' gallery. In the world of light railways, too, one name stands supreme, that of Holman Fred Stephens. Like the others he too was an engineer, but unlike them his reputation rests as much on his administrative ability in running railways as on his engineering skill in constructing them. A visitor to his offices at 23 Salford Terrace, Tonbridge, Kent during the 1920s would not perhaps have been unduly impressed by the modest suburban terraced house, but the neatly lettered board by the front door would have left him in little doubt that he had reached the hub of a light railway empire. Here, it proclaimed in letters of gold, were the offices of the Kent and East Sussex Railway, the East Kent, the West Sussex, the Snailbeach, the Shropshire and Montgomeryshire, the Weston, Clevedon and Portishead, the Festiniog and the Welsh Highland Railways – and even that list covered only a portion of the railways with which Colonel Stephens was involved.

Holman Fred Stephens was born in 1868 into a world where one might have expected an interest in railways to be crushed rather than encouraged, for his father was Frederick George Stephens, art critic of *The Athenaeum* and a member of the pre-Raphaelites, a group not noted for its enthusiasm for the modern world. Young Holly – and how very odd it seems to think of the stern, upright military gentleman of later years ever being known by a nickname – showed no aptitude for art. He went to London University to study civil engineering, then to the Metropolitan Railway to study mechanical engineering. In 1890, at the remarkably young age of twenty-two he was appointed Resident Engineer on the 11½ mile long Paddock Wood and Cranbrook Railway in Kent. The line displayed many of the traits that were to distinguish Stephens' lines. Sharp curves and steep gradients proliferated, while the stations were of the simplest possible construction, little more than basic shelters of corrugated iron and timber. If any artistic spirit was inherited from his father then it never showed itself in his station designs. Economy was everywhere the rule, not elegance.

From this modest beginning, progress was rapid but steady. In 1895 he graduated from resident engineer to engineer and locomotive superintendent on the Rye and Camber Tramway in Sussex, to be followed by a similar post on the Chichester and Selsey Tramway. By 1898 when he joined the Rother Valley Railway he had added 'Managing Director' to his list of credentials and from then on his career was set.

By the end of the century he had supervised the construction, and often the running, of thirteen light railways and had even found time to fit in one waterway, when he was appointed engineer in charge of improvements to the Medway Navigation. The line with which he will always be most closely associated is the Kent and East Sussex Railway, formed by the amalgamation of the Rother Valley Railway and the Rolvenden and Tenterden Railway. It was on this line, at Tonbridge, that he had his own headquarters, and it was here that he ruled his empire. He also found time to work on other lines as consultant engineer, thirty-six of them in fact by the end of the Great War, and during that bloody conflict he raised and commanded a troop of over 2,000 men and 220 officers. He returned from war in 1916 with the rank of Lieutenant Colonel in, inevitably, the Royal Engineers, and was to remain Colonel Stephens for the rest of his life.

So how did this extraordinary man keep control of and organise his railway kingdom? The short answer is, by taking a personal interest in everything that went on in all his various domains. It was his habit to descend unannounced on any station anywhere in the group – or perhaps one should say the visits were meant to be unannounced. Colonel Stephens travelled by train around the system and word of his progress generally preceded him, so that his visits were never quite the surprises he intended. Not that it would have been easy to keep plans of his movement secret, for the colonel not only liked to travel by train but he liked to travel in style. He bought two special coaches for his own personal use, not just ordinary coaches but royal saloons, originally built by the London and South Western Railway for the use of Queen Victoria. By the time the colonel

acquired them, they were well past their prime, the more elderly of the two having been built in 1844 and the other in 1852. They had been improved and modernised over the years, but both showed their venerability in the sweeping curves of the stagecoach type doors. They also retained their aura of grandeur and were kept in immaculate condition ready and waiting for one of the famous surprise visits. Of course the demand for the coaches from head office removed part of the element of surprise and a word on either of the two railways where the coaches were kept – the Kent and East Sussex and the Shropshire and Montgomeryshire – put everyone along the line on their best behaviour. All, however, seemed agreed that the colonel was scrupulously fair in his judgement of what he saw on one of his royal processions. Shortcomings were all noted and those responsible very soon received a decidedly sharp note, full of dire warnings of what would happen if matters were not speedily set to rights. Equally, however, good work received its reward in words of praise, hand outs of first-class cigars from what appeared to be an endless supply, and even handsome tips. The latter were always welcome, for pay on the light railways generally lagged behind the rates paid on the main lines.

The stately, imperial progress of Colonel Stephens around his various concerns was more than just a way of helping the boss to keep in touch with works and workers, it was also a way of demonstrating that those at the top were not too grand to be concerned about the vexations and problems of running a railway. There is, however, a fine distinction to be drawn between concern and meddling and there was a good deal of the autocrat in Stephen's personality. Those who sinned against the rules could expect little mercy. His employees soon learned the the various signs by which his mood could be judged. When he appeared with his hat sat square upon his head, then fine weather was in prospect; but when it was pulled down low over his eyes, it was time to hoist the storm cones.

The organisation of the different lines was all directed from the terraced house in Tonbridge. There were a dozen clerks employed there, each allocated on a particular line. They had responsibility for the administration and accounts, though it cannot have been an easy matter to control a railway in Shropshire from a base in Kent. Office work could be centralised, but the day-to-day business of running a railway ultimately had to depend on the people on the spot. Different companies had different policies on various points, but on one thing all Stephen's concerns were unanimous – economy was the keyword. It spread through everything, starting with such basics as the purchase of locomotives and rolling stock. If Colonel Stephens had not been a successful British railway man, then he could well have made a fortune in an eastern bazaar, for no one ever struck a harder bargain. He rarely bought new and what he bought was as likely to be third-hand as second-hand. Not that this was unusual on light railways where cost cutting was a constant preoccupation, but few could match the bargaining skill of Stephens. Some scarcely tried. Daniel Young, of the Wantage Tramway, was sent up to Crewe to examine an old London North Western tank engine which he declared to be satisfactory and passed back to the directors at Wantage the information that the asking price was £350. The board made a lower offer and received this curt reply from Crewe: 'With reference to yours of yesterday, when we ask a price it is the one we intend to take; and as you have not been able to make up your mind, the engine is now under offer to other parties.' Collapse, as the Victorian cartoonist would say, of stout party: the £350 was sent off by return. Colonel Stephens would not have given in that easily.

Buying cheap was one essential ingredient of success: making the most of what you bought was another. This meant that improvisation had a certain part to play in the running of a line. Neither freight traffic nor passenger traffic were able in the majority of cases to make a line solvent by themselves. In fact, there were frequently neither sufficient goods nor sufficient passengers to make even one train profitable. Consequently mixed trains were the order of the day, with all that involved in terms of elaborate shunting at each and every station. On those lines where freight predominated, such as the East Kent Railway which never ran more than one passenger coach per train, freight inevitably had the upper hand. When the goods waggons were fully laden, the engines would huff and puff up the steep gradient to Eastry South station, and the driver knew full well that if he stopped he would never start off again. So on he would go, ignoring the shouts and curses of frustrated passengers waiting on the platform not to mention those already on the train who had been hoping to get off there. Not surprisingly, passenger traffic on the line declined rather more rapidly than goods. Colonel Stephens, apart from being a locomotive bargain hunter, was also a man more than willing to investigate alternatives to the conventional steam locomotive. At the beginning of the 1920s he began the experiments that were to lead to the use of rail-buses on the line. The first trial was with a second-hand Wolseley-Siddeley car chassis – even with his bolder experiments Stephens could not resist going for a bargain.

What an extraordinary object it was. The chassis and the engine under its conventional bonnet looked familiar enough, but the railway wheels looked decidedly odd and stranger still was the omnibus top stuck on a chassis that was far too short to contain it, so that the end of the carriage stuck out alarmingly into space. It was not an unqualified success, though it did the round of the Stephens lines before losing its motor and being converted into a more conventional coach, which was used for inspection trips and was usually headed by the tiny locomotive *Gazelle* on the Shropshire and Montgomery. Even when its travelling days were ended, the coach was still kept in service, now reduced to the role of permanent way line hut. Right to the end, the Stephens economy measures ruled.

The first experiment was, however, sufficiently successful for the development to be continued and it culminated in the building of the grandly named 'Duplex Rail Motor Cars'. These bizarre objects consisted of two vehicles, each with a driving position and omnibus type carriage, coupled back-to-back so that the set could be driven in either direction without the need for shunting. Grand the name might have been, but the rail motor set quite failed to live up to the grandeur of their title. Breakdowns were frequent, and it was not unknown for a passenger to look out of the window to catch the somewhat alarming sight of one of the wheels bouncing off along the ballast. Clutch and engine failure was commonplace, and many passengers finished their journeys by taxi at the company's expense. This was no doubt a welcome relief, for the ride was notoriously rough on the rail cars and the carriage seats were uncompromisingly hard. In one sense the rail cars were a failure, but they were undoubtedly

cheap to run and in the depression years of the thirties that could mean the difference between survival and closure. On the Kent and East Sussex Railway, the rail cars rattled up nearly 180,000 miles during the years 1929-37 – which represents a little over half the mileage put in by conventional steam locomotives – and that is a very significant contribution indeed.

Economy lay at the heart of all Stephens enterprises, and economies were built into the system from the first. Lines were laid out with great sweeping curves to avoid unnecessarily steep gradients – which the venerable locomotives that were the norm on these railway might not have been able to climb. The official speed limit was never passed – seldom, indeed, reached – so that it was considered perfectly safe to do away with such niceties as gates at level crossings, thus saving the expense of employing crossing keepers. Other cost savings were effected by throwing out all the old established railway practices and demarcations. If you worked for Stephens, you had to be prepared to turn your hand to anything. The work was hard and the pay low, and there was no union to argue for better conditions, for anyone who attempted to organise a union branch was instantly sent packing. Many who joined these railways left of their own accord after a few weeks – others stayed throughout the life of the railways.

As with staff, so too with passengers. There were some who loved the quirkiness and character of the light railways – even if it did not always appear that all light railways were equally fond of their passengers. The by-laws of Wantage Tramway, for example, seem mostly concerned with listing all the people they would not carry, a list which included drunks, travellers with diseases, those with dirty clothes that might soil the upholstery, and all smokers. For those passengers who loved railways, there were an equal number who found their slowness and waywardness hopelessly irritating. On one thing, however, all were agreed: the working life of a light railway was very different from that of the great trunk routes of Britain. And some lines did at least put passengers first, not simply lumping them in with the parcels as a necessary but unwelcome part of the business of making a railway pay.

The Snailbeach District Railway was a mineral line, that served lead mines in the area of Shropshire, near Stiperstones and Pontesbury, where lead ore was transhipped on to the main line network. Here we see the locomotive depot at Stiperstones, with the derelict lead mine in the background. Kerr Stuart locomotive 0-4-2 tank, number 2, runs light past the shed, with one of the two Baldwins and the remains of Bagnall 0-6-0 tank *Dennis* outside, c 1930. (*Photographer Unknown*)

Locomotive number 2 hauls a long train of empty four-wheel hopper waggons, on the way back to Stiperstones. The Snailbeach District Railways were opened in 1873 and were originally owned by the same company associated with the Glyn Valley Tramway. After the First World War, the lead mining industry was in decline and the railway too went into decline, closing in 1915. Colonel Stephens took over the line in 1922 and his company, operated the concern until the 1950s, when Shropshire County Council leased the line to extract road stone. (*Photographer Unknown*)

Snailbeach Baldwin 4-6-0 tank number 3, runs light past the sidings at Pontesbury, c 1930. Colonel Stephens took over two locomotives in poor condition in 1922. As a result of this two ex-W D, Light Railway Operations Division, Baldwin 4-6-0 tanks were purchased as replacements. The two Baldwin's and the Kerr Stuart tank were then used until the line ceased to be locomotive operated in the late 1940s, when a Fordson tractor was used to haul the wagons. (*Photographer Unknown*)

The loading platform at Pontesbury, with hopper waggons waiting to be unloaded. The standard gauge open waggons were shunted underneath the loading platform, for the narrow gauge hopper waggons to be placed above to have their loads discharged, c 1930. (*Photographer Unknown*)

The 3 foot gauge Rye and Camber Tramway was opened on 13 July 1895, from Rye to Golf Links and was extended to Camber Sands on 13 July 1908. The tramway largely served the golfers at first and then also served the many holidaymakers who visited the sands in summer. Here we see the terminus at Rye, with the station building and rolling stock sheds in the background. The tram is made up of both the tramways carriages, the Bagnall and Rother Iron Works vehicles. The locomotive is Bagnall 2-4-0 tank, *Victoria*, c 1924. (*Author's Collection*)

Cutting the first sod, on the North Devon and Cornwall Junction Light Railway. This line opened on 27 July 1925 and was one of the last new light railways constructed in Britain after the First World War. The North Devon & Cornwall Junction Light Railway connected Torrington with Halwill Junction, and filled a gap in the network in the border area between Devon and Cornwall. The gentleman in the suit and hat on the far left is Colonel H. F. Stephens, the famous light railway engineer and promoter. (*A. M. Davies*)

The other end of the line at Camber Sands, with the Kent Construction Company four-wheeled petrol tractor, nicknamed 'the lawn mower' and the Bagnall carriage. The petrol tractor was acquired by the tramway in 1925, as a back up to the two Bagnall 2-4-0 tank locomotives, *Camber* and *Victoria*. As a result of the introduction of the petrol locomotive, the smaller Bagnall 2-4-0 tank, *Camber*, was withdrawn in 1926. (*Photographer Unknown*)

The Rother Valley Railway opened to traffic on 2 April 1900 from Robertsbridge to the first Tenterden station, later renamed Rolvenden. The line was extended up the 1 in 50 incline to Tenterden Town on 15 April 1903 and finally extended to Headcorn on 15 May 1905, together with the change of name to Kent & East Sussex Railway. The company had plans for extensions to Rye, Pevernsey, Cranbrook and Maidstone, none of which came to fruition. Hawthorn Leslie constructed 2-4-0 tank number 1, *Tenterden*, stands at the head of all the company's new carriage stock, six four-wheeled carriages and two brake vans, at the first Tenterden station in March 1900. The four-wheeled carriages were later reconstructed as three bogie vehicles, two bodies to each bogie underframe. This is an interesting picture, depicting a new light railway before official opening. Note the early locomotive shed, with round top roof and the basic water tower. (*Author's Collection*)

Hawthorn Leslie constructed 2-4-0 tank, Kent & East Sussex Railway number 2 *Northiam*, at Rolvenden shed on 19 August 1933. Number 2, *Northiam*, was the second Hawthorn Leslie locomotive delivered to the company in 1900, for the opening. This locomotive was hired to Gainsborough Pictures in 1937, for the making of *Oh Mr Porter* on the Basingstoke and Alton Light Railway, and posed as the locomotive Gladstone in the film. (*H. C. Casserley*)

Locomotive number 3, formally *Bodiam*, crosses the road at Rolvenden with a train for Headcorn on 14 August 1937. This locomotive was purchased from the London Brighton South Coast Railway in 1901, to provide extra motive power for the line, and was formally L B S C R Stroudley A 1 class, number 70, *Poplar*. (*H. C. Casserley*)

Ex-North Pembroke & Fishguard Railway and Great Western 1380, descends the 1 in 50 incline from Tenterden Town to Rolvenden, with a single non-corridor ex-L S W R bogie carriage, on a Robertsbridge service, c 1932. Manning Wardle, constructed in 1880, became Kent & East Sussex Railway locomotive number 8 after its purchase from the Bute supply company in 1914. This 0-6-0st was named *Ringing Rock* on the N P & F R and retained the name after purchase by the K & E S R. It was however renamed *Hesperus* at a later date. (*H. C. Casserley*)

A1X Terrier 32655 arrives at Tenterden Town station with a train from Robertsbridge in the summer of 1953, less than a year before closure to passenger traffic, on 2 January 1954. This scene depicts a light railway in its last months of existence, at the sunset of an era in Britain's transport. Note the three arm lower quadrant signal, a unique feature at this station. (*E. C. Griffith*)

O 1 class 0-6-0 tender goods 31370 stands in the platform at Tenterden Town station in the winter of 1949, with a train for Rolvenden. The O 1 class were the main class of locomotive used on the Headcorn extension, from the 1940s onwards, replacing the plethora of Kent & East Sussex and Southern hired locomotives from before and after the Second World War. (*Lens of Sutton*)

The Brighton Stroudley Terrier class 0-6-0 tanks were a feature of the Kent & East Sussex line, from 1901 when number 3, *Bodiam*, was purchased by the Rother Valley Railway. The original company owned two Brighton Terriers, numbers 3 and 5, which gave good service to the railway over many decades. The class continued to operate on the line well in to British Railways days, both during and after the line closed to passenger traffic in 1954. Here we see a Southern A1X Terrier on hire to the original company, with a train from Headcorn, near Tenterden St Michaels, with a single carriage train for Tenterden Town. (*L C G B, Ken Nunn Collection*)

Most of the light railways managed by Colonel H. F. Stephens were eccentric and quirky affairs, with some strange choices of rolling stock. Perhaps two of the most unusual carriages, on any British light railway, were the two former Royal Saloons, acquired by the colonel from the L S W R. The carriages were originally acquired by the colonel for use on the P D & S W Jc Rly in Cornwall. They were both sold on to the Kent & East Sussex Railway and the Shropshire & Montgomeryshire Light Railway. Both vehicles were nearly preserved: the K & E S R carriage was acquired by the Southern Railway for a planned museum but because of the Second World War, the historic vehicle was scrapped, its body surviving until the 1960s as a grounded body in Kent. The second carriage which was on the S & M R, was inherited by the army in the Second World War and used as an inspection saloon. After the war, the intension was to transfer the carriage to Longmoor in Hampshire for museum preservation, however fate again took a hand and this important vehicle was also broken up, due to a rotten body. Here we see the Kent & East Sussex Railway example number 10, at Rolvenden Yard, c 1930. (*Author's Collection*)

The East Kent Railway was opened in stages from November 1912 to 1925, when the railway had two lines, one running out to Canterbury Road, 11 miles from Shepherdswell, and a branch from Eastry to Richborough Harbour, 4 miles, which only had a limited passenger service to Sandwich Road until 31 October 1928. The stations and infrastructure on the line were rather basic, as can be seen in this picture of Eythorne Station taken on 5 August 1937. (*J. W. Sparrow*)

If ever the term, 'it's better to travel than to arrive', had any truth, then whoever coined the phrase was probably thinking of the station at Wingham, Canterbury Road. Canterbury Road was on the road to Canterbury and was nowhere near anywhere of importance. The East Kent Railway did have aspirations to extend to Canterbury, but alas lacked the finance to do so. As a result of this the line ended in a field, pointing in the direction of that great city, as we can see from this picture, taken in June 1939. Not surprisingly this section of the East Kent Railway was the first to close after nationalisation, passenger traffic ending on 30 October 1948 and freight on 25 July 1950. (*Rev A. W. Mace*)

The Millwall Extension Railway was an example of a city based minor railway, serving the docks in the North Greenwich area of East London. Here we see one of the company's Manning Wardle 2-4-0 tanks, heading a train of ex-Great Eastern four-wheeled carriage stock, at North Greenwich station, c 1905. The company later replaced these small tank locomotives and carriage stock with ex-Great Western steam rail cars in the 1920s. The line finally closed to all traffic in 1926, after the general strike. (*Author's Collection*)

Chapter Four

Sea, Sun And Scenery

One of the features of the spread of railways had been the development of the seaside holiday: the railways brought the crowds and resorts such as Scarborough prospered. So, if a large resort could grow into a great resort with help from a major railway, might not a little resort develop into a large one with the help of the light railway? The promoters of both railways and resorts certainly thought so and made every effort to prove their case – with somewhat mixed results.

Mr E.B. Ivatts, manager of the Lee-on-the-Solent Railway, was quite convinced that the little village of Selsey on the end of Selsey Bill in Sussex was destined for great things, and that all that was needed was a rail connection to the London, Brighton and South Coast Railway at Chichester. Selsey was described as a 'pretty and unconventional resort' much favoured by the legal profession, where the family could be taken for the summer while father commuted to London. The suggestion for the railway was put forward in 1895, meetings held in 1896, and by 1897 work was under way, with two locomotives already on order from Pecketts of Bristol. The main obstacle confronting the builders was the Chichester Canal which, since it carried sailing boats with tall masts, had to be crossed by a moveable bridge. The cost of the drawbridge was carried by Chichester Corporation who then leased it to the railway at a peppercorn rent of

£2 per year. On 27 August 1897, little more than six months after work had begun, The Hundred of Manhood and Selsey Tramway was duly opened. Even by light railway standards this was an eccentric line. At the opening, the mayor of Chichester insisted on driving the engine, a job for which he possessed no qualifications whatsoever, and though he travelled on the footplate it is doubtful if he was ever allowed to do a great deal. The route was a pleasantly rural one, skirting Pagham harbour on an embankment, passing the golf course where there was a halt but no shelter, and running past the beach – another shelterless halt – to Selsey itself. The company had, it seemed, little faith in the reliability of their new locomotives, for although timetables were provided giving details of when trains would leave the termini, no hint was given of when they might be expected to arrive at the other end. This was perhaps wise for when such details were finally provided, it was rare for the times to be kept. This unpredictability at least endeared the line to the local children who – it was said – were never short of an excuse if they arrived late at school.

There was little reason to explain the wayward timekeeping, for the run was only 8 miles long and there were no signals to impede progress. There were, however, several ungated road crossings which were to prove a nuisance in the years after the First World War. The growing traffic in buses and motor cars was thought not to mix very happily with the railway, now renamed as the West Sussex Railway. So, at each crossing, the guard had to clamber down and march to the middle of the road waving a red flag by day and a red lantern by night. I was delighted to find this arcane practice still in use on the Train Touristique in Normandy, though I cannot vouch for the lantern. There was also the problem caused by single track working. If a train did break down, not, it seems, a rare occurrence on this line, then that was the end of the traffic until the track was cleared. A young lad was despatched on a bicycle to call at every halt and station along the way to inform any would-be passengers that services were over for the day.

The growing traffic on the roads did more than provide extra work for the guards; it also took away trade from the railway, and the West Sussex went the way of many another light railway. By 1931 it was bankrupt. Selsey never did develop to rival Bognor; perhaps there were never enough lawyers to keep the place busy. The days of the 'Selsey Bumper' were over: no more lobsters from Selsey to Chichester, no more buckets and spades from Chichester to Beach Halt.

A railway that in many respects epitomised everything that was most attractive – or most irritating, depending on one's point of view – about the seaside line was the Weston Clevedon and Portishead Railway. The history of the line proceeded not unlike the trains that used it, in a series of fits and starts. Portishead, Clevedon and Weston-super-Mare were respectively port, watering place and seaside resort and each had a rail connection. What they lacked were connections with each other. The connections were all made via branches off Brunel's Great Western main line, and the local citizens felt

that there should be a more direct route between the towns, just the sort of situation that could be met by a light railway. In fact, the first steps were taken when an Act was obtained for a tramway in 1885. This was to include a street tramway through Weston and an unusual bridge over the River Yeo, which would carry both the railway and a roadway on which tolls would be collected. These varied from a penny for foot passengers to sixpence for horsedrawn vehicles. Various persons were exempted from the tolls: members of the royal family who were passing that way were allowed to go free, as were policemen and any prisoner to whom they happened to be handcuffed at the time.

The law demanded that the engines should be clean and silent and they were limited to a speed of 8 miles an hour through the streets of Weston. It was all begun with high expectations, for there were prospects of a good passenger trade and a substantial freight trade from the Black Rock Quarry near Portishead. The Act allowed five years for work to be completed, but the five years passed, the money had run out and the line was far from complete. 1890 saw the passing of Act number two, which suggested some new thinking had been going on, for provision was made for electric traction. One year was allowed this time, but only 4 miles of track were completed, the cash ran out again and in 1892 Act number three appeared on the scene. By now the street tramway element in the scheme had disappeared from sight, and the line was to be one which joined the GWR at both Weston and Portishead: two years were permitted for the Weston–Clevedon link and four for the Clevedon–Portishead section. By now the fact that the official date for completion passed with little sign of completion actually arriving surprised no one. But, for once, work did at least continue and in 1897, somewhat belatedly, the first train ran from Weston to Clevedon.

Officials were then given a triumphal run down the line and the official inspector called in. He was not unduly impressed. There were no signals on the line, but the company announced that they proposed to have only one engine in steam so signals were not required. Trips so far had been on the contractor's engine, and when the inspector asked to see the company's own engines he was somewhat startled to discover that not only did they not have any, but there were not even any on order. He found many faults in the works and quite reasonably declined to authorise the beginning of public services. Work, however, was hastily put in hand to set matters right and, at last, on 1 December 1897 the first public train was set on its way – still drawn by the borrowed engine. The company did, however, soon acquire their own locomotives, two 2-2-2WT engines built by Sharp Stewart for the Furness Railway. Neither was in the first full flush of youth – the first to be delivered having been built in 1857 and the second in 1866. It was not perhaps a glorious beginning – but it was a beginning.

The company now turned its attention to the rest of the line, where again the time given by the Act had long since expired, and a certain amount of local opposition was now in evidence. Not everyone was overjoyed by the prospect of steam locomotives invading the peaceful countryside and the Clevedon locals were also a little concerned at the idea of the same locomotives chugging through the streets of their town. There was nothing for it but to go back to Parliament again. This time the tramway concept was dropped altogether and the company received the name it was to carry for

the rest of its working life: the Weston, Clevedon and Portishead Light Railway Company. This Act was passed in 1899 and yet another five year extension granted. And was that five years sufficient? Of course it was not. 1904 came and went and legal wrangles continued, mainly concerned with the controversial road crossing in Clevedon. Complex rules were drawn up, covering everything from a ban on whistling near the church (by the locomotive rather than the passengers) to a requirement for the level crossing gateman to walk in front of the train on his crossing. All parties were finally appeased, work continued and on Wednesday 7 August 1907, a mere seventeen years late, the first trains ran from Weston to Portishead. The company officials were exhausted, the money had all gone and within two years, the receiver had been called in and the line was placed under his control until the debts owing to the Excess Insurance Company could be paid. They never were. A number of managers came and went until in 1911 management passed to Colonel Stephens.

Was it all worthwhile? Did all those Acts and all that labour produce anything worth having? In strict financial terms, the answer has to be in the negative. The line never paid, but when it finally closed to traffic in May 1940 the crowds that gathered around the last train proved that if it had not generated profit, the railway had at least generated real affection. And that is not too surprising, for the line passed through some splendid countryside, which included the East Clevedon Valley, known locally as 'Swiss Valley'. The description was somewhat exaggerated, for the hills of Somerset were scarcely alpine. From the Cadbury Road halt, passengers could explore the ancient British site of Cadbury camp. The name, however, was not well received by the locals, who objected to their station being appropriated by the delvers into ancient history and who would have much preferrred to see it established as their very own Weston-in-Gordano station. These minor skirmishes only added to the general colourfulness of the local scene, and it is tempting to believe that the charm of the line percolated through the stately walls of Clevedon Court to infect young Arthur Elton who, as Sir Arthur Elton Bart, was to accumulate one of the finest collections of old railway prints and paintings in the world.

Like many a light railway, the WCPLR was to gain a reputation for waywardness and eccentricity. The historian of the line, Colin Maggs, quotes an incident where – and again this seems no more than familiar light railway malpractice – a clergyman and his wife were taken on past the station for which they had booked tickets. The unhappy pair complained, at which point the obliging driver reversed his whole train for several miles to the appointed spot. This is just the sort of quirkiness which I had always assumed was limited to light railways, except that in 1981 I was on a main line express from London to Dover which similarly missed out a station and was speedily reversed for several miles. Perhaps light railways were not so odd after all.

The character of the WCPLR was finally established by its role as a connection between seaside resorts – it was there to be enjoyed. And enjoy it the passengers certainly did. It was not a line for those in a hurry, little help to the harrassed businessman, but for those with time to spare it was a delight. The pace was slow, so slow that it was possible to go blackberrying without leaving the moving train. Accidents were rare and suitably bucolic, generally involving nothing more serious than a difference of opinion between a panting locomotive and a recalcitrant cow on the line. The railway was part of seaside fun, a holiday treat. The same can be said of another, and remarkably successful, sesaside route.

This is a line which owes its existence to a railway built to carry iron ore to the furnaces of Whitehaven in Cumberland. The link, however, is not quite direct, so perhaps we should start at the beginning with the opening of the 3ft gauge railway, built from the iron mines of Eskdale to Ravenglass. This was no more than one among many industrial lines, the fortunes of which fluctuated with the swings of trade. In this case, the fortunes of the line were tied to those of Whitehaven Iron Mines Ltd, but when that concern collapsed the railway was able to struggle on for a few years but succumbed – finally, it was presumed – in 1913. That should have been the end of the story, but a gentleman then appeared on the scene whose name is known to model railway enthusiasts the world over, Mr W.J. Bassett-Lowke. He had long had a dream of using miniature locomotives to work a proper railway. Here was a line whose commercial life as a goods line was clearly over but which ran from the coast up to Eskdale in the Lakeland fells. It was a wonderful opportunity to turn his dreams into reality. He leased the line, and the narrow gauge route was shrunk still further into a diminutive 15in gauge track. There was an unexpected bonus for the railway when Beckfoot quarries were opened in 1922, and for thirty years granite from the quarries was brought down to the coast by the railway which had already acquired its popular nickname, 'The Ratty'. When quarrying ended in the 1950s, the line looked set to follow many other light railways down the track to oblivion, and would have done so but for the enthusiasm of the line's admirers. A trust was set up, the railway was bought and kept running – and it still runs today. Passengers can still steam up through the beautiful woodlands and out on to the fell, drawn perhaps by *Prince Charles*, a 4-4-2 locomotive of 1912, built by Bassett-Lowke, and identical to Sans *Pareil*, the first locomotive to run on the 15in gauge. Here, for once, is a heartening success story, that was to be copied in southern England.

At first it seemed as if this southern route might follow a similar development pattern to that of 'The Ratty': stop, then go, with rather more stop than go. The idea of a light railway across Romney Marsh to join the South Eastern Railway station at Hythe with New Romney was mooted as early as 1899, when a Light Railway Order was approved. Papers were drawn up, prospects were discussed but nothing whatsoever was done throughout the next quarter of a century. Real action came through the efforts of two racing drivers, Captain J.E.P. Howey and Count Louis Zborowski, who rather liked the idea of running a 15in gauge railway for themselves on the Ratty model, and wanted somewhere to run it. The Romney Marshes seemed the ideal spot – the land was flat, it was a seaside area where a lot of people might be found who would think that a ride on a tiny railway would be a welcome change from sitting on a pebbly beach waiting for the sun to shine. By now the Southern Railway held an option on the route, but they were only too happy to relinquish it to Howey and Zborowski. In November 1925 a Light Railway Order was granted, the Romney, Hythe, and Dymchurch Light Railway was formed and work commenced. Count Zborowski was not to see the line completed, for he was killed in a motor race, but Howey went ahead and in

1927 the line was opened with two locomotives. *Green Goddess* and *Northern Chief*, both 4-6-2 locomotives by Davey Paxman of Colchester, are still in use. The line was a great success and was soon extended to Dungeness, providing a total running length of nearly 14 miles. The line has had its ups and downs, figuratively that is, for physically it is nearly dead level throughout its length. But it still keeps going, carrying holidaymakers and providing a service for local residents. School children are still sent with satchels and shining morning faces on the Romney, Hythe and Dymchurch Railway.

It is a fascinating experience to travel the line, for it is at the same time both a light railway and a true miniature railway. Everything along the way is a scaled-down version of the main line routes, and this is especially true of the locomotives which are like everybody's favourite toy train set grown up and set to work. How visitors view the route depends to a large extent on how they react to the curious, flat, windswept world of the marshes. There are certainly few features of great interest along the way, apart from the Royal Military Canal at the Hythe end. It is the sea and marshland that exert their own fascination, in spite of frequent eruptions of caravans and holiday chalets. The end of the line is perhaps strangest of all, for when Dungeness arrives it seems less like the end of the line and more like the end of the world. It is, I suppose, a matter of taste, and each year thousands of seaside visitors demonstrate that the Romney, Hythe and Dymchurch is very much to theirs.

Some lines not intended originally for the tourist trade nevertheless ended up depending on the holidaymakers for a good part of their revenue. The North Sunderland Light Railway started life as an ordinary industrial-cum-rural route, though perhaps at this point it should be made clear that it had nothing to do with Sunderland, the important port on the River Wear, but derived its name from North Sunderland, a tiny village on the Northumberland coast. So why was the line built? There were some hopes and expectations of a tourist trade and the prospectus for shareholders boldly announced that 'the picturesque features of the district round Seahouses and North Sunderland, the coast, and of the Farne and Holy Islands, must, with the facilities for reaching them which the new line will afford, inevitably attract a large visitor and excursion traffic during the summer months.' But the emphasis for the prospectus as a whole was firmly set on the fish trade. Tempting prospects were held out of great quantities of shell fish, white fish and kippers being sent out from the coast to the main line less than 4 miles away. Other traffic too was promised, including limestone – and the massive lime kilns still stand by the harbour at Seahouses as reminders that this was once a lucrative trade. In the event, however, it was the passengers who were to keep the line going, and this really should have come as no surprise. Is there a finer stretch of coastline in England than this, with its tall dunes, broad sandy beaches and ancient castles overlooking the sea, while just offshore are the islands, as beautiful as they are historically interesting? The short run off the main line in antique coaches drawn by equally venerable locomotives seems to us now as the best possible way of getting to the coast. But, sadly, in the days when steam had no novelty appeal and comfort was placed before quaintness, the public tired of the little trains and services came to an end.

Trains and the seaside do seem to go exceptionally well together, whether it is a case of jolly rides on narrow gauge lines such as Fairbourne or enjoying the grandeur of standard gauge travel. Today we mourn their passing for often they offered special delights. How sad that we can no longer leave the old Great Eastern main line at Halesworth to wander across the Suffolk marshes past the tiny village of Blythburgh, with its magnificent church telling a story of more prosperous times, across the river at Walberswick to the charm and elegance of Southwold. The Southwold Railway alas, is no more, though traces still remain, including the bridge at Walberswick, now used by pedestrians only. Perhaps Southwold lacked the more robust appeal of Lowestoft and Yarmouth, for the traffic never quite developed as planned. But a different sort of appeal was there and the line is still remembered with affection. So, the light railways to the sea enjoyed their moments of glory and assumed many forms. But before turning to other routes let us look at a line which brought all the elements together: conventional railway and light railway, standard gauge and narrow.

The inhabitants of Jersey were quick off the mark in their attempts to bring the island into the railway age. The first proposals were put forward as early as 1845 but collapsed under a barrage of claims of double dealing and chicanery. So, instead of being in the vanguard of railway progress, Jersey began to fade towards the rear. It was 1860 before proposals were again put forward for modest line linking St Helier to St Aubin. Progress now was to advance at the rate of an unusually lethargic sloth. A bill was prepared in 1861, extended in 1862 and agreed, with the exception of one complaint from one local shipbuilder, in 1863. It was thought necessary to consider the complaint carefully and a correspondence began on the subject between the governments of Jersey and England that was to last right through until 1869. At last, after a mere twenty-four years of prevarication, work could begin on the railway and the sea wall that was to protect it. The engineers proved rather more expeditious than the planners and politicians and in September 1870 Jersey's new railway was officially opened. Encouraged by finally having something tangible to see for their efforts, the railway enthusiasts of Jersey began planning new routes: notably the Jersey Eastern Railway and a line promoted by the ponderously titled St Aubin's and La Moye Railway and Granite Quarries Company Limited, a name which at least had the virtue of telling everything that needed to be known about the line – or almost everything. The line was to join the quarries at Corbiere Point to the existing railway at St Aubin. What was not clear at first was that it was intended to build the new line to a 3ft 6in gauge. Inevitably it seems, as with all matters relating to Jersey railways, things did not go smoothly on what was, in effect, an extension of the first railway, albeit with a change of gauge. The old company and the new company haggled, and the end result was the formation of an entirely new company, Jersey Railways, to run both lines. It was clear that a break of gauge suited no one so the old line was replaced and a narrow gauge ruled from St Helier to La Moye. There were to be other changes of ownership over the years, but at least the route was established.

The line was everything a seaside line should be. The original route swept round the wide arc of St Aubin's Bay before turning inland where, if the sea was no longer in sight, then there was splendid scenery by way of compensation. It passed, a contemporary account noted, 'upwards through a beautiful glen, giving alternate glimpses of precipitous rocks, green hollows, romantic cottages, slopes covered with fern and ivy, and broad expanses of furze and heather.' If it sounds like a wonderfully romantic landscape, then it also sounds remarkably like a landscape ill suited to railway construction, and in that description can be found the reason for the narrow gauge. The line twisted and bent round the humps and hollows in a way that would never have been possible with standard gauge. In this it was very like another line which went to the seaside, but also took in some splendid inland scenery – the Lynton and Barnstaple Railway.

By the end of the nineteenth century, Barnstaple was well served by rail, with both the Great Western Railway and the London and South Western Railway bringing tracks to the town. Not so very far away were the beautiful little seaside resorts of Lynton and Lynmouth. Surely one of those mighty companies would wish to extend their lines to the coast. The mighty companies looked at the possible traffic, noted that between Barnstaple and the coast lay the hills and deep valleys of Exmoor and politely declined. The Lynton and Barnstaple Railway Company was formed by local interests who felt that they knew better and proposed a 2ft gauge railway. Such a railway would, they very reasonably argued, be the only one that could cope with the terrain and it would in itself be an attraction. The Lynton and Barnstaple Railway was, in short, to be Devon's answer to the Festiniog Railway. The promoters were anxious to avoid the criticism that the railway would destroy the essential tranquillity of the seaside towns it was to serve and they proposed to make Lynton station 'invisible'. They succeeded in that aim but unfortunately, in doing so, they also made it inaccessible. Passengers were not amused to find that when they reached their destination they were 700ft above sea level, and a long way out of town. It was all very well going down to the sea, but it was a mighty long trudge back up again. They could, however, pay an extra charge and use the cliff railway that had opened for business in 1890, and is still at work today.

In terms of engineering, the Lynton and Barnstaple was a triumph, a little railway with features that would not have disgraced a main line: high embankments, deep cuttings and a fine tall viaduct at Chelfham. The gradients were necessarily severe: 8 miles at a steady 1 in 50 is a daunting prospect and there were even more severe grades, though these were shorter and could be charged at and rushed. The great disadvantage of the line, however, lay in its extravagant curves, forced on the engineers as much by the intransigence of local landowners as by the demands of the landscape. Passengers who had planned a boat trip when they reached the water often declared themselves to be already too seasick from the lurching railway to venture out on the waves. But it was a lovely line made even lovelier by one regular passenger, the Rev Chanter of Parracombe, who scattered flower seeds from the carriage windows as he travelled. If you walk the line today you will find it still rich in summer flowers. But for all its attractions, for all the grandeur of the scenery, the line could never be called a great success. Opened in 1898, it closed in 1935. Only a few years after opening, an article appeared in the *Pall Mall Gazette* deploring the intrusion of the railway into this quiet corner of the West Country, and lamenting the folly of the locals who had sunk their cash into the venture. It ended with a phrase that could serve as

an epitaph for more than one light railway: 'Running a railway is an expensive game for amateurs'. The message arrived too late to deter the promoters of what was scenically a superb line, but financially an unmitigated disaster.

The Leek and Manifold Valley Light Railway ran from the North Staffordshire Railway's line near the quarries of Cauldon Low up the valleys of the Hamps and Manifold to arrive at – nowhere. The terminus was the hamlet of Hulme End (although the original intention was to continue to join the LNWR line to Buxton) where the railway buildings and a local hotel soon became the most prominent buildings. Along the way, the line passed magnificent limestone crags to match those of Dovedale, but where were the passengers to come from? Those who came were in for a treat, for they could stop off at numerous halts, including one from which they could clamber up the hill to inspect the majestic Thor's Cave high above the line. The trouble was that few local people came at all, although there was considerable excursion traffic especially on Bank Holidays; for instance, during Whit week in 1905, 5,000 passengers were carried. For thirty years it struggled on, its main traffic being milk from the outlying farms, and when the dairy at Ecton closed the line finally succumbed, but its fate was not quite that of other lines. The route was still as fine as it had ever been, so the old track bed was covered in tarmac and turned from a railway track to a walking and cycle track, and so it remains. Where once you could have ridden in style behind an Indian-style narrow gauge locomotive, now you must use your own leg power to follow the same line. But as anyone who has used the track can testify, it does at least bear out one statement made by the line's promoters: the Leek and Manifold Valley Light

Railway offered its passengers a view of the Peak District at its best.

It often seems in looking over the light railway scene that the story is invariably one of lines opened in high optimism and closed all too shortly after in deep gloom. But it did prove possible for some companies to offer routes the attractions of which are so great that the customers are still paying today and look likely to be using the line for many years to come. The Vale of Rheidol Railway was officially begun with the passing of an Act of Parliament in 1897 though construction work did not start until 1901. It is a narrow gauge (2ft) line which at first was designed to fulfil two functions: to serve the mines in the hills above Aberystwyth and to take tourists to see the famous Devil's Bridge. Once this was a prosperous area, and the local lead mine made so much money for the owners that it was named 'Potosi' after the richest silver mine in the world. In time that trade diminished with the decreasing production of the mines, but through it all the tourist business thrived. Devil's Bridge had become established as a major attraction in the eighteenth century, partly because of its romantic name – for which no one seemed able to offer an explanation – and partly for the grandeur of the scene, the waterfall beneath the bridge dropping in a deep cleft to the valley floor. The English came in their thousands, somewhat to the bewilderment of the locals. George Borrow in his famous book *Wild Wales* published in 1862 described a meeting with a local landlord who told him: 'A great many English go to see the Devil's Bridge and the scenery near it, though I really don't know why, for there is nothing so very particular in either'. Certainly there is little that is obviously diabolical about the bridge, but the scenery really is quite splendid. And so indeed is the scenery viewed from the train as it hauls its coachloads of sightseers up into the hills. Rather than diminishing the attractions of the line the years have only served to increase them, for the splendours of the scenery are augmented by the delights of steam. The publicists, for once, have not exaggerated and this really is 'one of the great little trains of Wales'. The pleasures of the journey are what they have always been – the steam trip itself and the scramble down by the waterfall followed, by those who do not keep a close eye on the time, by an even more hectic scramble up again as the steam whistle announces an imminent departure.

One other Welsh line should be mentioned, though whether or not it qualifies as a light railway is open to question. The Snowdon Mountain Railway was begun in 1894 and is unique in Britain, a rack railway built on the Swiss Abst system. It is a genuine oddity in every sense, with the locomotives seeming the oddest part of all. They were built with sloping boilers so that when the gradient is at its steepest, 1 in 5.5, the water above the firebox remains level. Everything has a somewhat un-British air, not surprising considering that the locomotives, four of which were supplied when the line first opened, were all built by the Swiss Locomotive and Machine Works. The original rolling stock, however, came from Lancaster, only the later coaches of 1923 being Swiss. It does not really fit into any pattern of British railway building. It is a one off and its uniqueness no doubt explains much of its lasting appeal, plus, of course, the fact that it takes visitors to the top of Wales' highest mountain with no effort on their part. Looking at the railway today one cannot help seeing how the twin lures of steam and scenery have worked their magic yet again; and equally one cannot help looking back at the lines that have been lost. Sea, steam and scenery are the ingredients that might have saved many a light railway from closure if only they could have lasted a little longer. History, however, is full of 'if onlys', and little good can come of them. Many of the most attractive lines in Britain have gone, and most of them have gone irretrievably. There will be no more buckets and spades on the North Sunderland Railway, no more outings to Thor's Cave by steam train along the narrow Manifold Valley. A lot of tourists have lost a lot of fun. Elsewhere, a lot of communities have lost their railways altogether.

Opening day on the Hundred of Manhood & Selsey Tramway, 27 August 1897. The crowds are waiting for the first train to arrive and sample their first experience of light railway travel. This picture conjures up the excitement and optimism of the late Victorian public, at the opening of a new local railway. (*E. C. Griffith Collection*)

An important feature of the Selsey Tramway was the lifting bridge crossing the Selsey canal. Here we see a sailing vessel about to pass under the bridge, c 1897. (*E. C. Griffith Collection*)

The Shefflex Rail Bus crosses a road near Selsey, c 1928. Although these rail car sets were introduced on a number of light railways to save money, they were something of a false economy, as they were uncomfortable and would often smell of petrol, which permeated from the tank. Colonel Stephens was very fond of them, having sets of these vehicles on the Kent & East Sussex, Selsey Tramway and Shropshire & Montgomeryshire light railways. The public were not so keen, as a large number of would-be passengers deserted the light railway, as soon as a rival comfortable bus service started. (*Lens of Sutton*)

Manning Wardle 0-6-0st, number 2 *Siddlesham*, crosses the lifting bridge across the Selsey canal, hauling a train of two Falcon bogie carriages, c 1900. (*E. C. Griffith Collection*)

The Weston Clevedon & Portishead Light Railway, started life in 1897, as the Weston-super-Mare, Clevedon and Portishead tramways. The line opened to traffic on 1 December 1897, from Weston to Clevedon, having a road tramway extension in Weston that never opened to public traffic. The company's name changed in 1899, to that of the W C & P Lt Rly and was extended to Portishead on 7 August 1907, after which the railway operated as a town and rural light railway, serving the three towns along the Bristol Channel coast. Here we see the terminus at Portishead on its opening day, with a train in the station and much activity on the platform. (*Author's Collection*)

The W C & P Lt Rly was for most of its life, short of money and therefore relied on second-hand locomotives and stock. The scene depicts Dubs constructed 2-4-0 tank (ex-Jersey Railway) General Don, W C & P R number 1, *Clevedon*, at Clevedon station with a mixed train of a Midland Railway open waggon and two of the Lancaster Carriage and Waggon, American-style bogie carriages. Note the ex-Metropolitan Railway Jubilee four wheel carriage in the background on the right. One of these ex-W C & P Lt R vehicles is now preserved in the London Transport Museum Collection in Acton, West London. (*E. C. Griffith Collection*)

The large Drury rail car at Clevedon station, c 1937, towing the small Drury rail car trailer. This rail car was constructed in 1930 and trialled on the Southern Railway, who sold it on to the W C & P R in 1934. (*Local Postcard*)

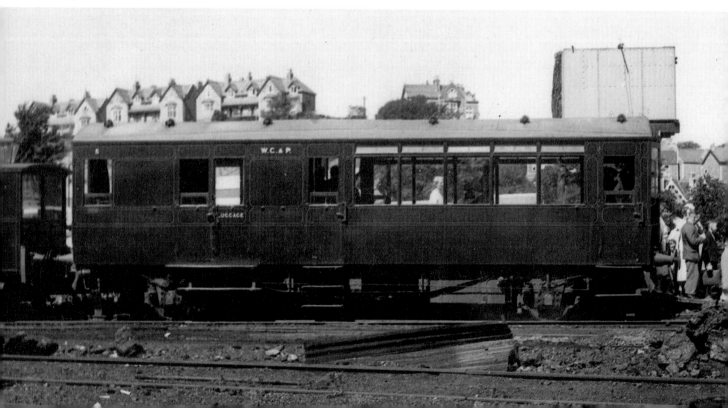

The W C & P Lt R became one of the lines managed by Colonel Stephens, from his office in Salford Terrace, Tonbridge in Kent. The colonel invested a small amount of money in the railway, including the purchase of Manning Wardle 0-6-0st number 5, which was constructed in 1919 and had disc driving wheels. Number 5 is being watered at Clevedon ready to depart with a mixed train of two ex-Metropolitan Jubilee four-wheel carriages and a string of open waggons, c 1925. (*Lens of Sutton*)

Manning Wardle 0-6-0st number 5, again with a mixed train of carriage stock, consisting of Lancaster American type stock and ex-Metropolitan vehicles, c 1930. (*Lens of Sutton*)

Ex-Furness Railway 2-2-2 WT, number 2, *Clevedon,* c 1903. Two of these old but handsome locomotives were purchased by the company in the early 1900s, being number 1 *Weston* and number 2 *Clevedon.* Both were replaced by newer, more suitable locomotives, before the First World War. (*Author's Collection*)

The Muir Hill petrol tractor in the yard at Clevedon, awaiting its next stint of shunting. This basic locomotive, another of the colonel's attempts to save some money, was purchased in c 1920s, for shunting on the jetty at Wick St Lawrence and for yard duty at Clevedon, c 1925. There was a second Muir Hill machine that resembled a garden shed on four wheels, which performed similar work. Both were scrapped in 1940, after the Great Western took over the line. (*A. M. Davies Collection*)

The Bideford Westward Ho & Appledore Railway was opened on 18 May 1901 and ran from Bideford quay to Appledore, via Westward Ho. This unusual standard gauge railway had three Hunslet constructed 2-4-2 tank locomotives, fitted with tramway skirts. All three locomotives were named; 1, *Grenville*, 2, *Torridge*, and 3 *Kingsley*. The railway which ran through the streets in Bideford, was more like a tramway then a railway, having centre couplings and balcony end bogie carriage stock. The line was not a financial success, being closed down on 28 March 1917, as part of the war economy during the First World War. (*Author's Collection*)

The Ravenglass and Eskdale Railway was opened on 24 May 1875, as a 3ft gauge line, promoted to serve the local stone quarries. The railway operated both passenger and freight traffic, relying on the seasonal tourist traffic, which was developing in the area at the time. The original 3ft gauge line closed and re-opened on two occasions and was finally taken over by W. Basset Lowke, who converted the line as a 15in gauge, miniature railway in August 1915. The railway today runs from Ravenglass to Dalegarth and is an important part of the local tourist industry. One of the Manning Wardle 0-6-0 tank locomotives, constructed in 1874, passes the Stanley Gill Hotel, with a single four wheel-carriage train, c 1899. (*Local Postcard*)

Manning Wardle 0-6-0 tank, *Devon*, stands in the platform at Boot station, with a train of four-wheel carriages, c 1910. The two original locomotives were both named rather than numbered, one being named *Nabb Gill* and the second named *Devon*. (*Local Postcard*)

The North Sunderland Light Railway was promoted by a syndicate, who constructed a number of light railways in the North East of England, including the Cawood & Selby and the Derwent Valley Light Railway. Opened on 1 August 1898, the North Sunderland Light Railway ran from Chathill, on the North Eastern main line, to Seahouses on the North Sea Coast. The railway only owned two locomotives in its life time, a Manning Wardle 0-6-0st, constructed in 1898, named *Bamburgh* and an early Armstrong Whitworth 0-4-0 Diesel shunter, constructed in 1934, named *Lady Armstrong*. *Bamburgh* heads a single four wheel carriage along the line, between Seahouses and Chathill, in this view, c 1935. (*Lens of Sutton*)

A newly delivered Armstrong Whitworth Diesel Locomotive, *Lady Armstrong*, stands in the platform at Seahouses Station on 9 June 1934. Both of the original locomotives were later replaced by motive power hired from the L N E R and later British Railways, who supplied Y7 0-4-0 tanks. (*H. C. Casserley*)

British Railways Y 7 0-4-0 tank number 68089 simmers in the corrugated iron locomotive shed at Seahouses in the spring of 1951, only months before the line's closure on 27 October 1951. Despite the nationalisation of the railways on 1 January 1948, both the North Sunderland Light Railway and the Easingwold Railway remained private concerns until closure. (*Author's Collection*)

The Southwold Railway was one of Britain's much loved narrow gauge lines, opened on 24 September 1879, and ran from Halesworth to Southwold in Suffolk. The line was constructed to 3-0ft gauge and was originally a smartly operated affair, with well-maintained infrastructure and a fleet of well-designed locomotives and rolling stock. Here we have locomotive number 3, *Blyth*, a Sharp Stewart 2-4-0 tank, constructed in 1879, at the head of a train waiting to depart for Halesworth, from Southwold station, c 1903. (*T. Middlemass Collection*)

A general view of Southwold Station, c 1910, showing the attractive buildings and track layout in the yard. (*Author's Collection*)

2-4-0 tank locomotive *Blyth*, shunts the yard at Southwold station, c 1912. The railway constructed a branch to the harbour, which was opened in 1915 and closed after a short period of use. The line finally closed on 11 of April 1929 and the company went in to receivership; all the railway's assets and rolling stock were left to go derelict and were not scrapped until the Second World War. (*T. Middlemass Collection*)

The two Sharp Stewart 2-4-0 tanks at Southwold yard on 10 September 1910. Both these locomotives were delivered in 1879 for the opening of the line, and served the company until closure in April 1929. The original locomotive number 1, *Southwold*, also a Sharp Stewart 2-4-0 tank, was sent back to the makers when the company found itself in financial difficulties. The original number 1 went a long way from home, and was sold to a railway in Central America, where it operated until the mid-1920s. The eventual replacement number 1 was also a Sharp Stuart product, a 2-4-2 tank constructed in 1893. It inherited the name *Southwold* and operated until the line's closure. (*L C G B Ken Nunn Collection*)

THE SOUTHWOLD EXPRESS   A COW ON THE LINE IS LUCKILY SEEN BY THE GUARD - IN HIS EAGERNESS TO STOP THE TRAIN HE PUTS THE BRAKES ON TOO SUDDENLY !

One of a set of amusing joke post cards, produced at the time of the lines closure in 1929. (*Author's Collection*)

Jersey Eastern Railway, Kitson constructed 0-4-2 tank *Calvados*, eases a train of four-wheeled carriage stock out of St Helier Station in the early 1900s. The locomotive has an ornate lined livery and the carriage stock is well kept and maintained in this turn of the twentieth-century picture. (*Photographer Unknown*)

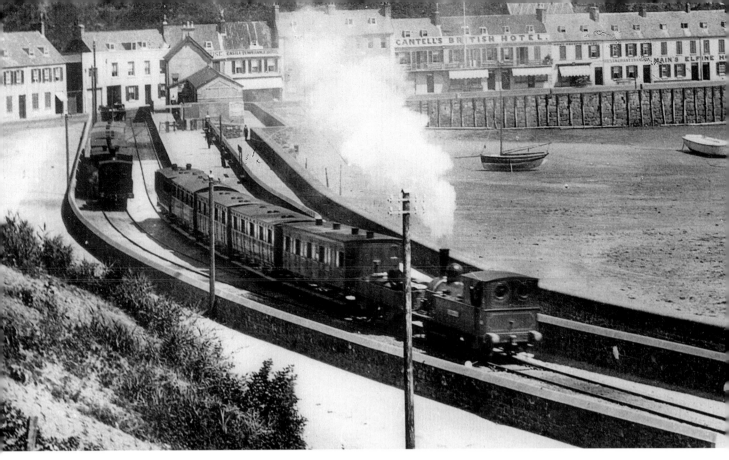

A Kitson 0-4-2 tank heads a train of four and six wheeler carriage stock, on a train at Gorey Pier station on the Jersey Eastern Railway. This panoramic view shows the station and its track layout to good effect. It also shows the road which sweeps past the railway station and continues around the quay on the far right. (*Local Post Card*)

Jersey Railway Company 0-6-0 tank number 4 and train of mixed carriage stock at St Brelades, c 1923. The Jersey Railway started life as a standard gauge line, like the neighbouring Jersey Eastern Railway, but was later converted to 3ft 6in gauge. The conversion took place in 1885, necessitating the complete reequipping of the entire railway's rolling stock and locomotive fleet. (*Author's collection*)

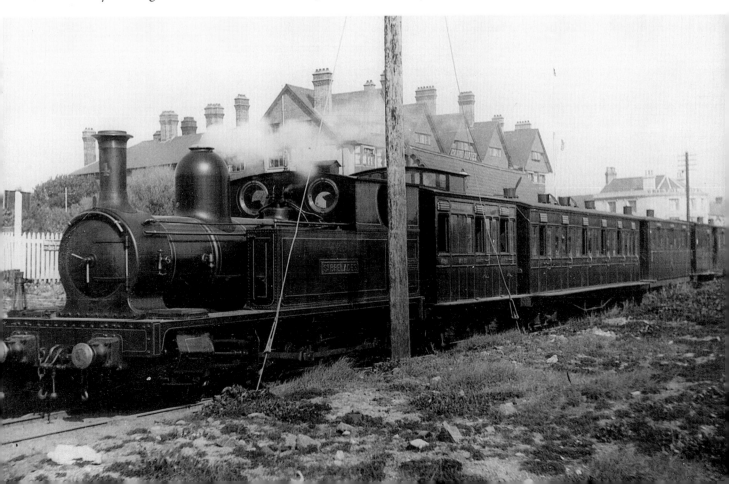

In the 1920s the Jersey Railway purchased two Sentinel steam rail cars, to try and cut costs. However this had little effect on the receipts of the line and both railway networks closed down in the mid-1930s. Here we see Sentinel steam railcar number two, *The Pioneer*, shortly after delivery in the 1920s. (*Lens of Sutton*)

The Lynton & Barnstaple Railway was probably one of Britain's best loved narrow gauge lines. Here we see one of the Manning Wardle 2-6-2 tanks running bunker first with a train to Barnstaple in the early 1900s. The line was constructed to 1ft 11½ inches and opened to traffic on 11 May 1898, becoming part of the Southern Railway on 1 January 1923. (*Author's Collection*)

Through the trees and along the hedgerows, this view of a train of four bogie carriages and a Manning Wardle 2-6-2 tank, on the Lynton & Barnstaple Railway sums up the romantic appeal of this lost period of Britain's light railways. (*Author's Collection*)

The last day on the Lynton & Barnstaple line, 29 September 1935, with a crowded train about to depart from Barnstaple Town station. It's a great pity the locals did not use the line, in the numbers that would have justified keeping it open. However the Southern Railway was just as much to blame as they never advertised it as a tourist attraction. A preservation society is now successfully reopening sections of this wonderful narrow gauge line and making amends for the Southern Railway's dismissive attitude. (*R. C. Stumpf Collection*)

A double headed excursion train for Lynton & Lynmouth heads over Chelfham Viaduct, c 1934, only a year before closure. Chelfham Viaduct was one of the important civil engineering features on the line and still stands today, as a permanent reminder of a once great English narrow gauge railway. (*R. C. Stumpf Collection*)

A second double headed excursion train headed by two Manning Wardle 2-6-2 tanks, the leading one being the last new locomotive constructed for the line in 1925, number 188, *Lew*. All the locomotives on the railway were named after local rivers; 759 *Yeo*, 760 *Exe*, 761 *Taw*, 762 *Lyn* and 188 *Lew*. (*R. C. Stumpf Collection*)

All the locomotives on the Lynton & Barnstaple were 2-6-2 tanks except number 762, *Lyn*, which was an American, Baldwin constructed 2-4-2 tank of 1899. The reason for the American locomotive was that during the late 1890s there was a locomotive famine in Britain, when demand for new machines outstretched the ability of builders to deliver. The main reason for this was the construction of a large number of locomotives for the British Empire, especially India, and the inability of builders to cope with new orders. Here we see the Baldwin 2-4-2 tank, number 762 *Lyn*, outside the sheds at Pilton yard in Barnstaple, c 1934. (*R. C. Stumpf Collection*)

Corporate vandalism at its worst. The smashed remains of some of the once handsome Lynton & Barnstaple bogie carriage stock at Pilton yard, c 1937. (*R. C. Stumpf Collection*)

The Leek & Manifold Light Railway was one of Britain's most interesting and beautiful minor lines, having the feel and look of an Indian narrow gauge railway, transplanted in the English country side. Its engineer, E. R. Calthrop, was responsible for the construction of the Bashi Railway in India, which was the same 2ft 6in gauge. The railway had a number of colonial features, including four balcony end bogie carriages and transporter wagons to take standard gauge wagons to goods yards along the Manifold Valley. Here we see one of the Kitson constructed 2-6-4 tank locomotives at Waterhouses station, with a connecting service, waiting for a train to arrive on the standard gauge North Staffordshire branch. The Leek & Manifold Railway was promoted as an independent company, operated by the North Staffordshire Railway and opened on 27 May 1904. (*Author's Collection*)

One of the Kitson 2-6-4 tanks hauls a train of bogie carriage stock for Hulme End, near Butterton Halt, c 1904, shortly after the line opened. The Leek & Manifold Railway had a very handsome livery of lined Madder red for its locomotives and bright primrose yellow for its carriage stock. (*Author's Collection*)

A Kitson 2-6-4 tank waits at Hulme End station, with a mixed train for Waterhouses, which includes a transporter wagon with a Midland Railway box van. In the background the locomotive and carriage sheds can be seen on the right, c 1928. The Leek & Manifold Light Railway was operated by the North Staffordshire Railway and became part of the L M S on 1 January 1923, closing on 12 March 1934. (*T. Middlemass Collection*)

One of the Leek & Manifold bogie passenger carriages in L M S days, with its colonial features, including its tropical pitched roof and balcony ends, c 1934. (*H. C. Casserley*)

Basic travel for the Manifold Valley, a pair of open sided bogie vehicles, made up from two of the Indian styled bogie freight wagons, c 1934. (*H. C. Casserley*)

The Vail of Rheidol Light Railway was opened as an independent company on 22 December 1902. The railway runs from Aberystwyth to Devil's Bridge, in mid-Wales and was originally constructed to 1ft 11½ins, to tap the lead ore traffic along the Rheidol Valley and provide a transport link for the tourist attraction at Devil's Bridge. The original company became part of the Cambrian Railways on 1 July 1907, before becoming part of the Great Western on 1 January 1923. The line lost its winter services on 1 January 1930 and closed for the duration of the Second World War, at the end of the 1939 season. Swindon constructed 2-6-2 tank locomotive 1213 waits at Aberystwyth, with a tourist train to set off for Devil's Bridge, c 1930. (*Author's Collection*)

Locomotive 1213 again hauls a Devil's Bridge bound passenger train of the later steel-bodied bogie carriage stock, near Aberffrwd, c 1938. The Vale of Rheidol reopened after the Second World War for the 1945 season, and continued to operate in the summer months, after nationalisation in January 1948, until becoming one of the first parts of British Railways to become privatised in the 1980s. (*Author's Collection*)

The Snowdon Mountain Railway operates the only steam rack and pinion railway in North Wales. The line runs from Llanberis to Snowdon Summit, a distance of 5 miles, and rises some 3,500ft above sea level. The line was opened in April 1896, closing almost immediately as a result of an accident forcing the railways suspension of services until the following year. The railway reopened in April of the following year for the new season and has operated each year ever since. The system of rack equipment and the locomotives are of Swiss origin, with eight Swiss locomotive works, Winterthur 0-4-2 tank locomotives, constructed to a gauge of 2ft 7½ins. Locomotive number 4, *Snowdon,* waits with a one carriage train for the road to the next block section, c 1904. The use of semaphore signalling on this line ended about 1930, the line operating using telephones and passing loops. (*Local Postcard*)

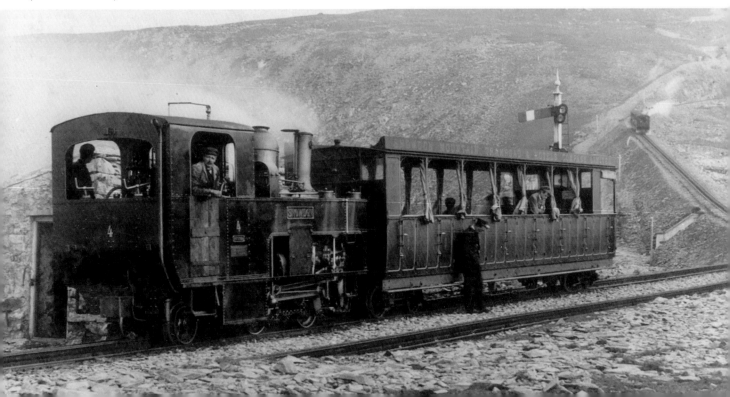

Chapter Five

Out In The Country

One of the great objects of the Light Railway Act was to open up rural Britain by the provision of railways. There were many problems to be overcome, however, before that admirable end could be achieved. Scott Damant of the Great Eastern Railway, writing at the very end of the nineteenth century, expounded the problems with admirable clarity:

> The chief difficulty in the way of providing light railways in the past has been the financial one. Obviously the districts where such lines would be a boon are poor, scantily populated, and devoted almost entirely to agriculture. Local landowners are, in such cases, seldom wealthy, and outside capitalists fight shy of providing the means wherewith to build a line between places they have never so much as heard of. A scheme for a light railway between Little Padlington-in-the-Slush and Great Hogwell-in-the-Mire is of vast importance to the enlightened inhabitants of those idyllic spots; alas! it does not appeal so forcibly to the hard-headed man of means with a partiality for a fair return in the way of interest on his investments generally.

Just what could be achieved with careful costing and good management was demonstrated by the promoters of the Wisbech and Upwell Tramway. Wisbech itself, as befitted a major trading port on the navigable Nene, had excellent main line connections through both the Great Eastern and the combined Midland and Great Northern routes. What was lacking was a railway that would plunge from Wisbech into the rich agricultural heartland of the Fens. It was the passing of the Tramways Act of 1870 which, though intended to ease the building of urban and suburban routes, gave the promoters a chance to build a rural tramway, though it might more accurately be described as a light railway with special features. It was the special features that gave the line its character.

The tramway was promoted by the Great Eastern Railway with the very sensible aim of collecting in agricultural produce from outlying districts which could then be fed into the main line network to meet the demands of more populous areas. The system had many advantages. For a start there was no need for a large administrative staff, since the affairs of the line could easily be attended to by the GER – and how many railways suffered under the excessive costs of bureaucracy; come to that, how many still do! Then, being a roadside route, the costs of acquiring land were slight – and those who tried to hold the company to ransom for a high price received no encouragement from the courts. Building was cheap, running was cheap – and aims were kept modest. It was not, perhaps, a recipe for those eager to make fortunes, but it was one well suited to the needs of the community.

Being a roadside tramway meant that the line and the locomotives using it had to meet a number of special conditions. The civil engineering was, however, straightforward enough with a line built to standard gauge over a flat landscape. The only obstacle to be overcome was the fenland waterways. Locomotion proved more of a problem. The Act laid down a number of rules and regulations including the following:

A governor, which cannot be tampered with by the driver, shall be attached to each engine, and shall be so arranged that any time when the engine exceeds a speed of fourteen miles per hour it shall cause the steam to be shut off and the brake applied.

Each engine shall be conspicuously numbered.

Arrangements shall be made enabling the Driver to command the fullest possible view of the road.

Each engine shall be free from noise produced by blast and from the clatter of machinery, such as to constitute any reasonable ground of complaint either to the passengers or to the public; the machinery shall be concealed from view at all points above four inches from the level of the rails, and all fire used on such engines shall be concealed from view.

The result of these regulations was a series of locomotives looking like sedately moving garden sheds: it was assumed they would not alarm the horses.

At first the line was as busy carrying passengers as freight, but inevitably road competition had its effect and the business slowly dropped away. It is sad to contemplate the end of those days, for there was a touch of elegance about the old carriages with their railed balconies – a pleasing contrast to the notable lack of elegance in the locomotives. But, unlike other similar routes, the end of passenger carrying by no means marked the end of the line. Freight carriage went on, reaching a peak at fruit picking time. The line was, in fact, providing just that service for which it had been built. And it went on providing it, moving on from the steam age to the diesel age, right up until 1966.

Other tramways developed in different ways, but one at least achieved an equal longevity and had quirks and foibles to match the Wisbech and Upwell. The Wotton Tramway, the Brill Tram and the Brill branch of the Metropolitan Railway: these are not three lines but one line wearing different names for different occasions, and the history of the line is as fascinating as any. No Act of Parliament was passed and no Light Railway Order was given for work to start on the Wotton Tramway, for it was privately built and privately financed by the Duke of Buckingham and Chandos. An enthusiast for railways himself, he decided to construct a line to join the main line at Quainton Road between Rugby and London, with his estates at Wotton. Noble railway builders had certain advantages over lesser breeds, for the duke not only owned most of the land over which the line was to pass but also had enough employees on his estate to build it for him. The original scheme was soon extended to bring the route up to the village of Brill. At first, it was intended simply as a freight route to be worked by horses, and the permanent way was laid on the Vignoles system with rails attached to longitudinal sleepers. The line was in use by the end of 1871 but it soon became clear that passengers also wanted to travel the railway. At first, only estate workers were allowed, but there was such a clamour from the locals that a carriage was added to the rolling stock. At this point the horses rebelled at dragging hordes of villagers and the railway entered a new phase.

The engine that was brought to the line in 1872 was not the familiar locomotive of the railways, but an Aveling and Porter traction engine adapted for tramway use. It had a single cylinder which drove on to a crankshaft with a large flywheel at one end. The drive to the wheels was by a chain and sprocket. Originally there was no cab, but complaints from cold and wet drivers persuaded the owners to provide some cover from the elements. The line was a success in that it took the products of the country on the way to the city and brought the products of the city to the country. In those days there were few things the city could produce that the country wanted. There was, however, one useful product. London, with its multitude of private carriages and public cabs, was a great source of horse manure. The fields around the Brill line benefited greatly, though the traffic may not have added to the appeal of passenger travel on mixed trains.

An attempt was made in 1873 to have the tramway officially recognised as a railway, but the Board of Trade inspectors would have none of it. The track was not up to the required standard and as the number of passengers being carried per day had by then dropped to single figures, they were quite unimpressed. So, the tramway went on its way. Many schemes were put forward for extending the line to Oxford, but none of them came to fruition. Ownership changed, but little improvement was noted in the track. Derailments were so commonplace that locals declared that a pail of milk despatched from Brill was likely to be cheese before it reached Quainton Road. Conventional locomotives took over from the old Aveling and Porter engines and in 1894 the line finally gained official acceptance under the ownership of the Oxford and Aylesbury Tram-road Company – a name born out of unjustified optimism concerning extensions of the route. Later, ownership was to pass on yet again to the Metropolitan Railway and, when that was abandoned in its time, to London Transport. Those who know Brill, the old brick-built village with its fine post mill on top of the hill, will cherish the thought of it as an outpost of London Transport. It was a splendid anachronism. London Transport, however, saw the anachronism, but not the splendour. In December 1935 the last train ran down the line to Quainton Road. The line has gone, but a few traces remain – a station house bears the initials 'B 6&. C 1871', a reminder of the noble patronage of Buckingham and Chandos. Thanks to the work of local volunteers, steam can still be seen at Quainton Road, now home to the Buckinghamshire Railway Centre, with an impressive collection of locomotives and rolling stock.

Many a rural line had a similar tale to tell of modest success, insecure funding and strange railway practices. Among those who could claim the latter, the Garstang and Knott End Railway in Lancashire, later renamed the Knott End Railway, would no doubt claim the prize for unorthodoxy. In a now familiar pattern, the line was promoted amid great local enthusiasm. Farmers looking for an outlet for their produce in the market town of Garstang were among the most enthusiastic, readily agreeing to provide land in exchange for shares in the company. Then the Act was passed, and doubts crept in. Was it really wise to give away land in the hope of some doubtful return? Some began to demand cash instead of shares, others changed their minds about which piece of land they were willing to hand over. The new company was born amid a flurry of legal wrangles – and legal wrangles are notoriously expensive. The result was that the line was only completed between Garstang and Pilling, and when that part was completed the route was so short that officialdom tended to ignore it and there was no check on safety standards.

The railway was originally worked without signals on the familiar one engine in steam principle. In fact, the line could only work on this principle since they only possessed one engine, which was required to work a very heavy schedule. This was acceptable enough, but the methods used for collecting rolling stock would never have been found in any respectable rule book. Waggons were simply left out on the line to be picked up by the advancing train, so that by the end of the journey there would be a respectable set of coupled waggons and coaches behind the engine. Whatever else had been collected along the way was pushed in front, generally uncoupled. This practice, which would have horrified any railway inspector, was a masterpiece of safe organisation compared with what went on at the goods yard.

The aim of the line had been to provide an alternative route for farmers who before had had to cart produce to market down dirty, twisting lanes. It was a success, but success brought its own problems. Every farmer in the area wanted, it seems, to make use of the railway to get his produce on the first available train. As there was not enough room for every farmer to achieve this, an unofficial allocation system sprang up. As the train of empty trucks appeared at the yard, the farmers would dash towards it and leap on to a moving truck. A farmer who got on to a truck could then claim the privilege of loading

it. That any responsible railway company could allow such a practice seems incredible, but if it was never officially approved, neither was it ever officially condemned – at least not by the company. It was condemned by the coroner after the first fatal accident – and again after the next, but it still continued and was only stopped when everything on the line came to a halt. The shortage of funds had finally caught up with the company and in 1872, just two years after the opening, the line was put up for sale. Not surprisingly, in view of its reputation, no one seemed eager to buy.

It took a good deal of work with the provisions of extra locomotives, new rolling stock and proper signalling to get the line out of its state of penury. The railway finally achieved its original objective of reaching Knott End at the mouth of the River Wyre. The rest of the story need not be told in detail. Fortunes rose – and fortunes slumped again. The line, having been extended from Pilling to Knott End, contracted back to Pilling again, earning the local service the name of the 'Pilling Pig'. Freight was found for the line and freight was lost again, and the last Pig snorted off down the line on 31 July 1963.

All these lines predated the famous Light Railway Act, designed more than anything else to promote the country railway. This it certainly succeeded in doing, and many rural routes were proposed, some of which were actually built. The Mid-Suffolk Light Railway will serve as well as any example. At the end of the nineteenth century, Suffolk was, in railway terms, a county with a great hole in the heart. This was not altogether surprising, for this was an area which could look back on a glorious past, but could offer no present which could guarantee profits to match those of the industrialised regions of

Britain. That the past had been glorious was witnessed by the great churches that then, as now, graced the villages. Their grandeur was based on a once thriving wool trade, but that had long since moved away, first to the West Country and then to Yorkshire. Nevertheless, a rich agricultural region remained, a huge tract of land skirted by the lines of the Great Eastern Railway – one route from Ipswich passing to the coast at Yarmouth, a second heading inland through Diss. This was just what the light railway doctor had ordered: an agricultural area that could be threaded by a railway that would join the two main lines. The Mid-Suffolk Light Railway was intended to cut right through the middle of this empty land, to join Haughley in the west with Halesworth in the east, a total distance of 42 miles. A company was formed in 1900, a Light Railway Order received in 1901 and on 5 May 1902, the grand opening ceremony was performed in the presence of an illustrious gathering who crowded round to applaud HRH the Duke of Cambridge as he cut the first sod. The ceremony was performed at Westerfield, which was somewhat unfortunate, for it was not only the first, but was to prove to be the last sod to be cut there, for the railway was destined never to reach the spot. The local paper paraphrased the words of a local writer, Edward Fitzgerald, translator of the *Rubaiyat of Omar Khayyam*, reporting that the company chairman had 'flung the stone into the night of Mid-Suffolk'. Would-be investors listening to the grand words about future profits might have been better advised to ponder another couplet of Fitzgerald's:

Ah, take the Cash in hand and waive the Rest;
Oh, the brave Music of a *distant* Drum!

The chairman himself, poor man, should certainly have heeded the warning for, after endless trouble with the contractors, numerous mistakes over the laying out of the line and many smaller, but still costly errors, three years went by, and he had sunk almost £100,000 of his own money into the venture with no end in sight. £10 shares were worth less than £3 and the unhappy chairman was declared bankrupt. Poor man, but poor railway too, for the bankruptcy proceedings revealed him as a hopelessly incompetent businessman who had shown as much sense in his handling of railway affairs as he had in managing his own. A man who buys jewellery on credit and then raises cash to pay his debts by immediately pawning it should not perhaps be trusted too far, even if, or the cynical might say especially if, he is the local MP.

The company struggled on without their chairman in rather better style than they had with him, but at the end of it all never succeeded in making the desired connections. At the western end the route left Haughley, staggered through various villages along the way, reached Loxfield, carried on a little further and then stopped: a line to nowhere. It should have been a simple enough line to construct and run, but even the best plans cannot survive a totally incompetent manager, and their first chairman, Mr Stevenson, was just this. The Mid-Suffolk worked out its days as a peaceful line along which the few passengers could travel at gentle pace through a gentle countryside. Perhaps given better handling more could have been made of it. Other lines started off under handicaps as great as those of the Mid-Suffolk and struggled through. Would things have been different if the concern had been in the hands of H.S. Stephens instead of F.S. Stevenson?

We saw something of the Colonel Stephens empire at work in chapter three: in particular the line which stood at the heart of his empire, the Kent and East Sussex Railway. Now we shall turn to one of the more distant outposts, the Shropshire and Montgomeryshire. Why this line rather than another? One could say that it showed the Stephens system for reviving lost causes in its most dramatic form, or that it has all the qualities one looks for in a rural line. But it has to be admitted that the true reason is that there was never a line which could boast a more varied and attractive mixture of locomotives. Serious historians will no doubt disapprove of such a frivolous reason, but the railway enthusiast will, I hope, understand. Before we get to the locomotives, however, a little of the history of the line must be inspected – and a remarkable history it turns out to be.

The line began with great aspirations, as companies dreamed of establishing Shrewsbury as a pivotal point from which lines stretched eastward to the manufacturers of the Midlands and west to the Welsh coast. The fact that Shrewsbury was already served by two mighty companies, the Great Western Railway and the London and North Western Railway, and that these were unlikely to offer much aid to late arrivals and rivals, seems not to have entered into anyone's calculations. Beginnings were modest enough with the formation of a small company whose sole objective was the sensible one of building a mineral railway to serve the limestone quarries of Llanymynech. Then ideas became enlarged, as did the company which expressed its larger ambitions in a new name, the Shrewsbury and North Wales Railway. Then agitation began in the east for a line to the Midlands, actively promoted by the North Staffordshire Railway. With one

interest looking for a route to North Wales and another to the Midlands it was decided to join forces to form the Potteries, Shrewsbury and North Wales Railway. This was known locally as the 'Potts'. Potty might have been a more appropriate name, for in spite of the grandeur of the title, the railway itself never reached any of the places named, apart from Shrewsbury. It went instead west out of Shrewsbury and only just managed to creep over the Welsh border to reach Llanymynech, with branches to Llanyblodwel and Criggion. The 'main line' was built as a double track, as befitted the aspirations of the company but scarcely the needs of the stations along the route: Red Hill, Hanwood Road, Ford, Shrawardine, Nesscliff, Kinnerley, Maesbrook, Llanymynech, though it should be mentioned that the latter provided a connection to the Cambrian Railways' line from Oswestry to Welshpool. This would, no doubt, have been a great boon to the citizens of these two towns who wished to visit Shrewsbury or send goods there, except that they already had rail connections before the Potts arrived. The best it could hope for was the local traffic, and the best hope of goods traffic came from the Nantmawr quarries. In what was to become typical Potts style, the Nantmawr extension was the last section to be built. It arrived too late to avert disaster.

The line was not cheap to build: there were considerable earthworks, bridges were needed to cross the existing rail routes centred on Shrewsbury and one rather grand six-span viaduct was needed to take the tracks over the River Severn. With all that money going out on the permanent way, there was little left over for stations. A brave start was made in Shrewsbury where Abbey Station, near a former abbey site, had station buildings of brick. Elsewhere there were simple wooden structures, not without a certain basic charm. In August 1866 everything was ready and the first train was duly despatched on its way. Five trains a day were announced: by winter it was down to four – an ominous beginning. Things were soon to get worse. In December, only four months after the opening, a debenture holder who had not been paid went to court and the court sent in the bailiffs. For a while, passengers had the company of the bailiff on every train that ran along the route. He occupied, somewhat warily, a first class carriage – warily because one of his brethren had been 'accidentally' shunted into a siding on the last train of the day and been forced to walk home. What could be done to raise money? The company took the somewhat dramatic step of selling off their locomotives and for two years nothing moved. By 1868 some confidence had been restored – somewhat misplaced in the event – and services restarted. They did not last long, as everything began to deteriorate. Journey times all but doubled and services were cut. In 1877 the receiver was called in and by 1880 everything had stopped yet again. And that, one might have expected, would have been the end of that. The years rolled by: trees and shrubs grew over the track, grass grew out of the station platforms and local youths used the remaining carriages for catapult practice. A new company appeared which promised to revive the route, but nothing ever came of it. The last of the assets were sold and the decay and rot continued. The nineteenth century passed away and still nothing had happened. Surely, it seemed it must now be admitted that all was finished. So it would have been had not the locals turned as a last desperate hope to the apostle of the new order, the fervent advocate of light railways, Holman

Fred Stephens. He looked at the line, and saw that it could never achieve its promoters' ambitions of becoming a main line, but saw also that it could have a future as a light railway serving local interests. The appropriate order was obtained, and in 1907 the Potts ceased to exist and the Shropshire and Montgomeryshire Light Railway was born.

The Stephens philosophy was soon to be seen at work on the line. Whatever could be saved was rescued, and where new work was needed it was done in the cheapest possible manner. Level crossings were swept aside, and no potential customer was ignored. Every single crossing became a halt, where local people could catch a train or load their produce. It was still a little line serving a remote country region, but Stephens firmly believed that railways that cut their costs to a minimum could be made to pay even in such unlikely areas. The company, rather more in hope than expectation, offered trackside sites for industrial development and, somewhat more successfully, establishing camping huts beside the River Severn. There was much emphasis in the advertising on the peace and tranquility of the region. It was, of course, precisely that peace and tranquility that had caused the first experiments to fail for lack of customers, but Stephens had enough sense to use the line's liabilities as an advantage. Excursions became profitable business; the camping huts thrived.

Everything that could be done to raise revenue was done, and everything that could be done to cut costs was also done – and that certainly included saving money on engines and rolling stock. Whatever the state of a locomotive brought in by the company it was dignified by a grand, often classical, name. Some of these names carried rather appropriate associations.

One could imagine the first two locomotives supplied, *Pyramus* and *Thisbe*, their names carrying echoes of Shakespeare's *Midsummer Night's Dream*, sitting comfortably with the 'rude mechanicals' of the engine shed. These were, in fact, supplied new by Hawthorn Leslie to a Stephens design, but proved too heavy for the track. They were replaced by the more usual Stephens breed of venerable cut-price engines from other lines. The replacement *Pyramus* was a Beyer Peacock of 1874, rebuilt in 1890 while the second *Thisbe* was a similar engine, but a year older. To these were added a classical trio of Terriers of similar vintage, dignified by the names *Hecate, Dido* and *Daphne*. These were all old but servicable engines with little out of the ordinary about them. But one locomotive in the ranks was far from ordinary: *Gazelle*, an animal the grace and speed of which was not matched by its mechanical namesake.

Gazelle was built as a 2-2-2 well-tank locomotive in 1893 for the personal use of the mayor of King's Lynn, who made arrangements to have it run over Great Eastern Railway and Midland and Great Northern Junction Railway metals. It was a tiny but bizarre engine, with wooden wheels and an open cab, behind which was a bench for four passengers. On arrival at the Shropshire and Montgomery Light Railway it lost some at least of its odder features. The wooden wheels were replaced by iron, set in an 0-4-2 configuration, a cab was added and the bench removed. It was – and is – a delightful little engine, with more than a touch of the absurd. The front end, with a shapely smoke box and tall chimney, looks well enough, but the cab is out of all proportion to the rest. It was used with an ex-London tramcar as a trailer for inspection work and occasionally for private charter. What a roaring trade the latter would

bring today, for who could resist taking this funny little engine out for a jaunt. That, alas, is no longer possible, but the engine survives in the National Railway Museum at York.

Somehow *Gazelle* seems to sum up the whole philosophy of the railway. It conforms to no known rational railway pattern, but it worked and engine and railway alike inspired true affection among all who knew them. Other engines were added to the stock over the years and a variety of rail buses were tried on the line. What must it have been like to travel on such a railway? Passengers arriving at Abbey Station could never have been very certain about the sort of conveyance that was to carry them on their way. Knowing travellers would have kept a very close eye on the make up of the rolling stock, for mixed trains were the order of the day and the greater the number of goods trucks and waggons, the longer the delays for shunting along the line. The coaches were as great a mixture as the locomotives and you could find yourself travelling in anything from a common ex-Midlands third-class carriage to something altogether grander, for very occasionally the royal carriage built for the London and South Western Railway in 1848 was pressed into service. This fine old coach was to have a working life that lasted for more than a century.

The motley collection of trucks and carriages would get under way but would scarcely have time to reach the maximum allowed speed of 25mph before it was slowing down again for the first stop at Shrewsbury West, for the occasional passenger to get on or off and the train get under way again for its next three-quarters of a mile dash to Moel Brace. Here were sidings and a junction with the Welshpool Line, which would almost certainly entail a long stop while the intricacies of shunting were practised by the railway staff, detaching some parts of the train and adding others. So it would continue: stop, go, stop, go to the end of the line 18 miles from the start which might be reached on a good day in an hour, though it was unwise to rely on that.

The railway was to be somewhat shaken out of its even course in the years of the Second World War, when it was taken over by the War Department, renewed with military enthusiasm and run with a military precision unknown even in the days of Colonel Stephens. War ended and the railway returned to civilian life, and a gradual run down of services ended in closure in 1962. It had begun with a troubled life, but it had ended by doing a good day's work and doing it well. No one could have asked more of it than that.

The Wisbech & Upwell Tramway was promoted and opened by the Great Eastern Railway on 20 August 1903. The line ran from Upwell Basin to Wisbech as a roadside tramway, to provide a freight and passenger service for a rural agricultural community. The trains were operated by Great Eastern constructed 0-4-0 tram engines made at Stratford works, in East London. From the mid-1950s, Drury constructed 204hp 0-6-0 diesel mechanical shunting locomotives operated the services on the branch. The line operated a passenger service, using specially designed balcony end, bogie tram carriages, which were also used on the Tollisbury branch. The passenger service was withdrawn by the L N E R, on 1 January 1928. Thereafter only freight trains worked on the line until 20 May 1966, when the line closed to all traffic. Tram engine 0125, waits at Wisbech with a mixed train for Upwell Basin, c 1920. (*T. Middlemass Collection*)

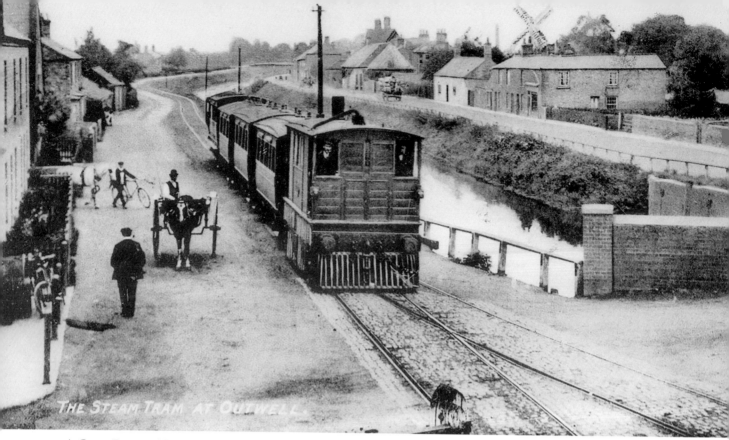

A Great Eastern Tram engine hauls a passenger service through Outwell, c 1905. The carriage stock had a low profile next to any main line freight or passenger stock, as can be seen from this picture. Both the steam tram engines and the later diesel replacements, had tram skirts fitted in order to prevent scaring horses or any livestock. (*Author's Collection*)

Manning Wardle 0-6-0st number 1 *Huddersfield* stands at the head of a mixed train for Brill, at Quainton Road station, c 1901. The Brill Tramway started life as the Wotton tramway, opening on 1 April 1871 and being promoted by the Duke of Buckingham. The tramway was originally constructed with lightweight rails and rough timber sleepers as a freight only operation, to transport timber and farm produce from the duke's estate. The line had four 0-4-0 geared, chain drive locomotives without skirts, as the tramway was on private land. Two of these machines were constructed by Aveling & Porter of Rochester and two by W. G. Bagnall of Stafford. The geared locomotives were very slow and were replaced with former contractors Manning Wardle 0-6-0st *Huddersfield* constructed in 1878 and later two newer Manning Wardle 0-6-0st locomotives, constructed in 1894, *Wotton* and 1900, *Brill*. The newer Manning Wardle 0-6-0st locomotives were later taken into Metropolitan Railway stock, when the line was leased from the original company. (*Author's Collection*)

A mixed train leaves Quainton Road station, with a service for Brill, in the mid-1920s, headed by Metropolitan Railway A class 4-4-0 tank number 23. The Brill Tramway was reconstructed in 1894 and leased to the Metropolitan Railway from 1 December 1899. In accordance with the terms of the lease, the Metropolitan Railway operated the line on behalf of the original company, providing locomotives, rolling stock and maintaining the tramway. (*J. H. L. Adams*)

Through the trees and onward to Brill, a Metropolitan A class 4-4-0 tank number 41 approaches Wood Siding on 27 August 1932. The line had a reputation for its rural idyll and many people, enthusiasts and general public, made a point of travelling on this rustic, bucolic backwater. Unfortunately, after the London Passenger Transport Board was formed on 1 July 1933, a very different view was taken and within 2½ years, the tramway was closed. The closure took place on 30 November 1935, after which the line was handed back to the original company for demolition, which took place shortly after. (*F. M. Gates*)

A class 4-4-0 tank number 41 again, this time at Brill, while running around its train. This is an interesting photograph, showing the locomotive shed and the adjoining buildings, including the various stores and workshops, which by this time, on 27 August 1932, were out of use. There were only two A class 4-4-0 tanks in service by this time, number 23, which is at the London Transport Museum, Covent Garden, London, and number 41, which unlike number 23, had lost its condensing pipes. (*F. M. Gates*)

The station at Brill, in the last year, with an ex-Metropolitan rigid eight wheeler carriage at the timber platform, with the station bill boards displaying modern London Transport posters. The buildings on the tramway were of a rather basic design, as one can see from this picture. It is said that the light railway promoter, Holman Fred Stephens, formed most of his ideas for designing light railways from trips on the Brill Tramway. (*S. W. Baker*)

Thaxted station, on the Great Eastern Thaxted branch, which was opened as a light railway in 1913. This posed photograph was probably used to publicise the new local branch line, which the Great Eastern Railway obviously hoped would be a lucrative success. The Great Eastern, like a number of other main line railway companies, made good use of the Light Railways Act 1896, constructing a number of light railways including the Thaxted and Tollisbury lines. This picture typifies the light railway scene of the pre-Great War period, with the neat simple station, low timber faced platform, with a gravel surface. The grounded six wheeler carriage body and the oil platform lamps are a typical feature of the rural stations on the Great Eastern. Perhaps the inclusion of a Model T Ford is an ominous sign of a not so bright and prosperous future. (*Local Postcard*)

The Garstang & Knott End Railway was opened on 14 December 1870. The company had a very shaky start, with the line opening and shutting within the first year of traffic on the railway. The rural nature of its location had a profound effect on the company's revenue, making its future shaky from the beginning. The railway managed to keep going until the grouping in 1923, when it became part of the L M S group. The picture depicts, Manning Wardle constructed 0-6-0 tank, *Knott End*, on a train of new balcony end, bogie carriage stock, at Preesall station shortly after the extension to Knott End on 29 July 1908. (*Author's Collection*)

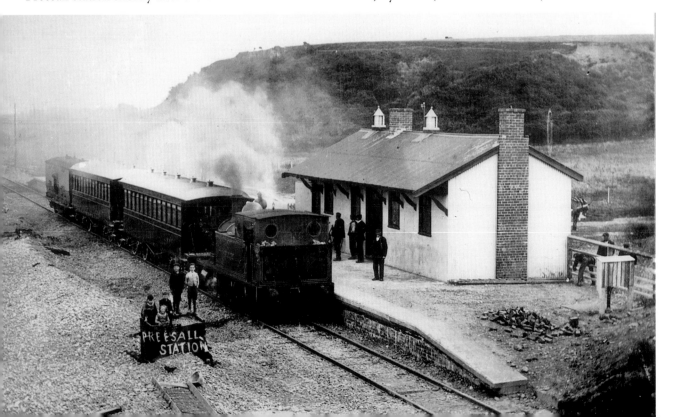

A large locomotive for a small railway, *Blackpool* was a Manning Wardle constructed 2-6-0 tank, out shopped in 1909. *Blackpool* was one of the most unusual light railway locomotives of all time, being, if anything, overpowered and large for a line like the Garstang & Knott End. In its own way *Blackpool* was both good looking and somewhat ungainly, with its long lanky front end and its small undersized coal bunker, looking like a machine that should have been a 2-6-2 tank. Despite the fact that *Blackpool* was only 15 years old, the L M S decided to withdraw the locomotive in 1924 and cut her up, without trying to find a buyer. (*Author's Collection*)

The Mid Suffolk Light Railway served a very rural, agricultural area in East Anglia and was like so many railways of its kind, a hand-to-mouth concern. The railway opened on 20 of September 1904 and linked Haughley to Laxfield, a small town in the middle of rural Suffolk. The company had constructed a temporary freight only branch in 1903, from Kenton to Aspall Road, on private land, which only functioned for a year. A further extension for freight was opened in 1906, from Laxfield to Cratfield, which only lasted until 1912. Laxfield is not far from Halesworth and it was always the Mid Suffolk Light Railway's aim to extend to Halesworth and connect with the Southwold Railway. Sadly this never came to pass, and the railway was still only operating its trains to Laxfield when the grouping took place in 1923 and the Mid Suffolk Light became part of the L N E R. Hudswell Clarke 1905 constructed 0-6-0 tank number 3, stands at the head of a cattle train, c 1919. (*T. Middlemass Collection*)

An early posed picture, probably at the time of opening, c 1904, with one of the Hudswell Clarke 0-6-0 tank locomotives and one of the four ex-Metropolitan four wheeler carriages, purchased for the opening, 1st 3rd composite number 2. This picture shows the Westinghouse air brake equipment on the Hudswell Clarke 0-6-0 tank to good effect. (*T. Middlemass Collection*)

The station at Aspall in 1951, only a year before closure, showing a lonely station with an empty platform. This picture shows the basic corrugated iron buildings and no frills nature of the infrastructure on most British light railways. The Mid Suffolk Light Railway never made much money for either the original company or the L N E R, so it was not surprising that, after nationalisation, British Railways decided to close the branch, which took place on 26 July 1952. (*T. Middlemass Collection*)

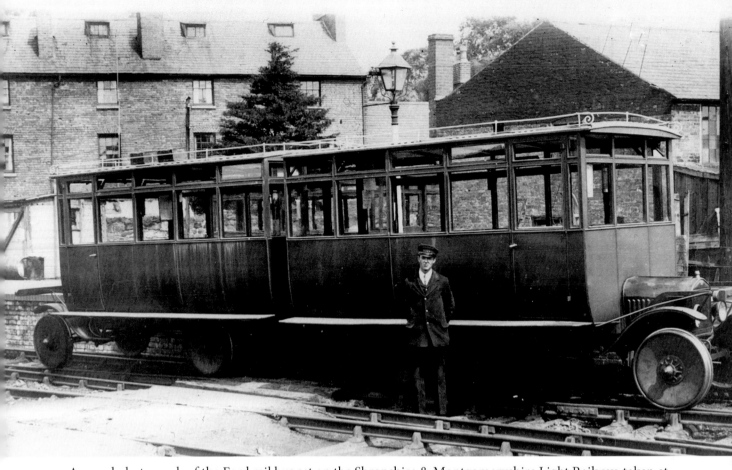

A posed photograph of the Ford rail bus set on the Shropshire & Montgomeryshire Light Railway, taken at Shrewsbury Abbey station, c 1926. This set originally ran as a three car unit, with a centre car, which was later removed. (*T. Middlemass Collection*)

A contractor's 0-6-0st runs over the viaduct at Shrawardine, on the Shropshire & Montgomeryshire Light Railway, c 1910, during the reconstruction of the line. The S & M started life as the Potteries Shrewsbury & North Wales Railway and was opened in 1866. The original company never made a profit and went bankrupt in 1880. Shrawardine viaduct was one of the main pieces of infrastructure on the line, which ran from Shrewsbury to LLanymynech, with a branch from Kinnerley Junction to Criggion, where a quarry was served. (*Author's Collection*)

74409

Kinnerley locomotive shed, c 1938, with an ex-L N W R 0-6-0 tender goods, awaiting its next turn of duty. The S & M had three of these locomotives purchased second hand from the L M S in the early 1930s, to replace older worn-out machines that had been acquired for the reopening in 1911. (*Lens of Sutton*)

Not a fare-paying passenger, but a local cow gazing across the empty platform of a halt on the Criggion branch, c 1938. (*Author's Collection*)

One of the most unusual locomotives in Britain, 0-4-2 W T, *Gazelle*, S & M number 1, at Shoot Hill with a special train, on the way to Kinnerley from Shrewsbury in 1939. *Gazelle* started life as a 2-2-2 W T in 1893, being constructed by Dodman of King's Lynn, a traction engine manufacturer for a wealthy enthusiast, who was a director of the Great Eastern Railway. *Gazelle* ran all the way to York on one occasion, on one of its original owner's trips, later sold to T. W. Wards of Sheffield. The small locomotive was sold to Colonel Stephens, who used the locomotive with an ex-L CC horse tram, on the Criggion branch. The horse tram body was later replaced with an ex-Wolsley Siddley railcar body in later years, as seen here. *Gazelle* is now preserved in the Colonel Stephens Railways Museum in Tenterden, Kent. (*R. S. Carpenter collection*)

Gazelle at Kinnerley yard, c 1925, showing the tiny locomotive to good effect. Note the bunker cab, which had seats inside for four passengers and the large centre splasher, from when the locomotive was a 2-2-2 W T, all giving the machine the look of a Victorian toy wooden engine, escaped from a nursery. (*Author's Collection*)

The former Royal Saloon, S & M number 1A at Kinnerley, c 1935. This vehicle was the sister carriage to the Royal Saloon on the K & E S R number 10. It is believed that Queen Victoria originally used this saloon to travel on the L S W R, on her journeys to and from Osborne on the Isle of Wight. This carriage was originally earmarked for preservation. However, due to severe body rot, the vehicle was broken up in the 1950s. (*H. F. Wheeller*)

Railway inspection and platelayers, pump trolley, on the S & M, c 1935. (*Author's Collection*)

A banner signal on the platform of a station on the Shropshire & Montgomeryshire Light Railway, c 1925. These banner signals were used to stop trains at wayside stations, being operated by the staff or passengers, using a hand lever to put into stop or pass position. The signal is seen in stop position. (*Photographer Unknown*)

Two ex-Great Western, Dean goods 0-6-0 tender locomotives, at Hookergate sidings, c 1946, awaiting cutting up after withdrawal from War Department service. The Shropshire & Montgomeryshire Light Railway was taken over by the War Department in 1940, for use as a military railway connecting store and ordnance depot, which were constructed along its entire length. The use of the line by the military continued until 1960, when they handed the line over to the Western Region of British Railways, for official closure and demolition. (*Lens of Sutton*)

Chapter Six

Serving Industry

Great numbers of purely industrial lines were built in Britain, but here we are only concerned with those which were built to light railway standards and which also carried passenger traffic – even if that was not always the original intention. It could be argued that this subject, rather than being tucked away behind seaside and rural lines, ought to be at the vanguard of any railway story. After all it was an industrial line, built to carry coal from collieries to a navigable river that first developed as a passenger carrier and user of steam locomotives – the Stockton and Darlington Railway. Or one could go back even further still and point out that it was on a mineral line, the Penydarren Tramway, that the steam locomotive first proved its worth. These are all valid points, but the Light Railways Act, from which so many of the lines glimpsed in this book developed, was not intended primarily to meet the needs of industrialists but rather to satisfy the demands of rural communities. Nonetheless, industry was to prove an important stimulant to light railway construction, and our first line shows how one railway can trace within its history almost the whole story of light railway development. The early tramways of South Wales were frequently built to join mines and iron works to the canals. In North Wales, early developments were chiefly concerned with the movement of slate. The owners of the Glyn Ceiriog slate quarries found themselves in a position that combined the two elements. The Ellesmere Canal, later to be known as the Llangollen arm of the Shropshire Union Canal, was completed in 1803. It ran from Llangollen down the Dee valley, but then turned south to cross the River Ceiriog at Chirk on a fine stone aqueduct. It must have been tempting to attempt to make a connection between the slate quarries and the canal at Chirk, especially as a connection had been made with the Dee valley quarries, and boat loads of slate were sent off every day for the roofs of England. But temptation was resisted. Nothing happened. Nothing happened again when a viaduct appeared alongside the aqueduct at Chirk carrying the rails of the Great Western Railway. Things did begin to move, however, in the 1860s when the Cambrian Slate Company decided to make a big effort to exploit Glyn Ceiriog slate and called in the services of a young engineer, Henry Dennis, who had worked on the Llangollen tramway.

His first plan was for a steam tramway that would run alongside a new turnpike road, but Parliament, faced with the notion of a road and railway being developed together had a fit of nervousness and tossed the idea out. Many another scheme was to rise and fall over the next few years, but with the passing of the Tramways Act of 1870, which gave official blessing to the street tramway, the first idea was revived. The Act itself was not invoked but its stipulations were followed – notably that rails should be laid level with the road surface and that horses, not steam locomotives, should be used for traction. The Glyn Valley Tramway Act was approved in 1870, though the thinking behind it seemed to belong to 1770. Some interesting decisions were taken. First, the gauge: that was set at 2ft 4¼in. An odd measurement, but 2ft 4¼in is exactly half the standard gauge of 4ft 8½in, though why that should be thought desirable remains a mystery. Then the construction involved one rope worked incline, half a mile long, down from the slate quarries, and in its final run into Chirk the line took on a steep gradient, much of which was at 1 in 30 but did rise as steeply as 1 in 19. This was very much the old tramway thinking, and to complete the sense of *déjà vu*, the running of the whole concern was entrusted to the Shropshire Union Canal Company. The one novel feature was the section that ran along the turnpike road. Work was finally completed in 1874 after nearly two decades of argument.

For fifteen years the ropes on the incline whirred round the winding drums while horses plodded the 9 mile route. From the very first, passengers were carried on the line, not always with complete safety. In December 1874 a truck left the rails at a sharp bend and deposited its four passengers into the Ceiriog. Later investigation showed firstly that the truck was running downhill under gravity without the use of a horse, and secondly that the brake man who was theoretically controlling the descent was drunk as a lord. There were many expressions of horror at this dangerous practice of running trucks under gravity without the use of a horse, and it was banned. It certainly sounds alarming – but it was a practice that was common on other lines as we shall see later. Most passenger journeys, however, were undertaken in more sedate manner behind a gently ambling horse,

which gave the travellers ample opportunity to enjoy the valley scenery. A touch of romance was provided by the post horn sounded by the driver at every halt. New traffic soon appeared on the line in the form of granite from other local quarries, a traffic that was soon to have even more importance than slate. One result of this increase in freight traffic was the ending of passenger services in 1886. These years also saw a change of management, as the Shropshire Union Canal Company withdrew, sold out its interest and left everything in the hands of the Glyn Valley Tramway Company. In 1879, a new Tramway Act had approved the use of steam haulage on street tramways, and the idea of replacing horses on the Glyn Valley Tramway now began to receive serious consideration.

The success of steam on other narrow gauge railways in Wales, following the experiments on the Festiniog, gave added impetus, and in 1885 a new act was obtained authorising reconstruction of the line to make it suitable for steam locomotives. In 1888 the new line was ready, though the gauge had mysteriously widened by a quarter of an inch, and soon passenger traffic was restored on the Glyn Valley. The horse tramway had become a steam tramway and it was to remain in use carrying passengers and freight until closure came in 1933. It was built as a mineral railway and most of its profits came from freight, but the passenger carrying service proved very useful to the local community and also brought visitors to the lovely Ceiriog Valley. Had the line still been open today it would, no doubt, be a thriving concern.

The Corris Railway was similar to the Glyn Valley in many respects, though it followed a more usual pattern for North Wales in taking slate from quarry to seaport. It was begun in 1858 as the Corris, Machynlleth and River

Dovey Tram road, a 2ft 3in gauge horse tramway. It easily beat the Glyn Valley into the steam age when it was reborn as the Corris Railway, but the line to the sea was abandoned when the standard gauge railway reached Machynlleth. The line that remained ran down the Dulas valley and a regular passenger service was established between Corris and Machynlleth in 1883. What a delightful run it must have been. A familiar tale, however, was soon to be repeated as the fortune of the company declined, the motor bus taking over passenger services in 1931 while the collapse of the slate industry led to final closure in 1948. For the last eighteen years of its life it had formed part of the Great Western Railway. That is not quite the end of the story. The Corris Railway, like the Glyn Valley, had double appeal – the appeal of steam and the appeal of running through some remarkably fine scenery. It is this that has ensured that the line is not yet forgotten, for the Corris Railway Society has kept a part at least of the old line intact, runs trains again and has plans for future extension. A near neighbour to the north has fared even better.

The Talyllyn Railway was, like the previous line, built to carry slate from a quarry in the hills to a port, in this case Tywyn. It is unlike the Corris in that, from the first, it was built for use by steam locomotives, and was also intended to be a passenger carrying line. Construction of the 2ft 3in gauge line was authorised in 1865 and a year later it was ready for inspection. It ran for 6¾ miles, climbing steadily from Tywyn to Abergonolwyn high in the hills. This marked the end of the steam line and the passenger line, but the route itself continued via two cable worked inclines and a level horse worked section to the quarries of Bryn Eglwys. So the line existed

in two parts: public narrow gauge railway and private horse tramway. The former is the one that concerns us here.

The inspection of the line proceeded in September 1866, but all, alas, was not well. In particular, the provisions for passenger carrying were considered quite inadequate. One feature that caused concern was the narrowness of the bridge openings. The inspector H.W. Tyler described the problem:

> The Bridges over the line have a span on the square of only 9ft. 1 in. or 9ft. 1½in. and the only passenger carriage which has yet been purchased is 5ft3½in. wide outside measurement. This leaves but 1ft 11in. between the outside of the carriage and the abutments, instead of 2ft. 6ins. which there ought to be. Mr McConnel, the Chairman of the Company, proposes to obviate this difficulty by permanently fastening the door and barring the windows on one side of his carriages and slewing the rails so as to allow sufficient space between the other side and the abutment. The objection to this course is that if a carriage was turned over on the unbarred side, with the barred side uppermost, the passengers would be unable to escape from it. But it must be admitted that this objection has not the same force in the case of a line of this description, on which only one engine will be employed for passengers and minerals at a speed intended to be no greater than 10 miles an hour.

It does seem a somewhat bizarre solution to the problems of passenger traffic, but it is nowhere near as odd as the picnic specials that were to be run on the line in later years. This is unquestionably one of the most dramatically scenic routes ever built in Britain and there is obvious appeal in the notion of travelling up the line for a day in the hills. That was fine, but how were passengers to get down again? It was a long walk and the last train to Tywyn left at what seemed to many to be an unreasonably early hour. The first printed timetable shows no trains from Abergonolwyn after 5pm. Then someone noticed that the ride from Tywyn was uphill all the way and therefore it must follow that the ride back would be downhill. So waggons were hired out by the company which could take a family up the line, after which they were detached and left until everyone had had their fill of mountain scenery. At that point the family would clamber back on board, release the brake and bowl merrily back down the line again. Needless to say, this practice did not receive official approval from the railway inspectorate.

The happy families bounding down the mountainside in their unsprung trucks rattling over a somewhat irregular permanent way represented only a fraction of the passenger traffic on the line. The main business was for many years quarry business. The men went up at the start of the week and returned at the end, spending the time between in the quarry barracks. There was not much fun in their travel, especially in winter when they made trips in unlit, unheated carriages. This is a line which displayed a Jekyll and Hyde character. Seen in one aspect it was a rugged mineral railway which also carried the work force, if in less than luxurious conditions. From another point of view it was a scenic pleasure route, there to be enjoyed. The former provided the whole reason for its construction, but it was the latter that ensured its survival. Today it exists purely to give pleasure to visitors, a story we shall be looking at in more detail in the last chapter. But it was always worth remembering that for most of its life this was a hard working, industrial

line. The distinctive slate waggons were of far more importance than the one-sided coaches. That has all changed, yet amazingly the two original locomotives built for the line are still in use, even though Tyler was unhappy about them when he wrote his first report in 1866.

No. 1 *Talyllyn* was described as being subject to 'vertical motion' due to its short wheel base. It was an 0-4-0ST and it apparently bounced along the rails in an alarming fashion. This problem was solved by the addition of a pair of trailing wheels, converting it to the present 0-4-2 configuration. No. 2 *Dolgoch* was an 0-4-0WT, which suffered from the problem associated with the 'boxers' on the Festiniog Railway: it swayed from side to side. This was said by Tyler to be due to an excessively long crank pin. The company promised to do something about it, but as there is very little you can do about it without redesigning the entire cylinder-crank arrangement, the promise remained unfulfilled. After well over a century's use it now seems to be accepted that perhaps no great harm will come from these oscillations after all.

The story of industrial light railways in Wales is one of a long past coupled with what one hopes will prove to be a prosperous future. Names such as Corris, Festiniog and Talyllyn are better known now than at any time in the past, even if the function of the railways has changed quite dramatically. When we come to look at England, a very different picture is seen. How many recall the working of the Cleobury Mortimer and Ditton Priors Light Railway, or can recall the busy life of the Ashover Light Railway? But not all is consigned to history books, the study of yellowing timetables and faded photographs. One at least of these lines is still in use – and not even as a preserved railway run by enthusiasts, for it is part of the everyday working of the British rail system.

This is the story of a company that built a main line route, acquired a narrow gauge mineral line and joined the two by a light railway. The area is the Tamar valley, which in the last century was a rich industrial region, the river banks being lined with extensive copper and arsenic mines, while the river itself carried a heavy trade on the distinctive Tamar sailing barges. It is also a story of many companies, and therefore a little complex. So let us start somewhere near the beginning with Brunel bridging the river to bring the broad gauge down into Cornwall, hoping to establish a Great Western monopoly in the region. Indeed, all the companies which built lines west of the Tamar in the early days were soon absorbed into the GWR empire. Then, in 1876, the London and South Western Railway ran their first train from the London terminus of Waterloo down into Plymouth and plans were laid to join this to the other LSW line which had reached Lydford. The proposal for the connection was made by the Plymouth, Devonport and South Western Junction Railway, which received the necessary authorisation from Parliament in 1888 and duly completed its undertaking.

By this time, yet another company had appeared and was running tracks down by the Tamar. The Callington and Calstock Railway ran, not surprisingly, between those two places and its change of name in 1872 to the East Cornwall Mineral Railway accurately defined its function. It was built purely and simply to carry the minerals from the mines of Callington and Kelly Bray to the quay at Calstock. But as anyone who has visited the area will know, the banks of the Tamar are high and steep, so that the river bank could only be reached via an

800ft long incline that dropped down 350ft. It was a profitable little plan and it dropped into the PD & SWJR lap in 1891. It was a self-contained narrow gauge route, but it offered the SWR the opportunity to gain another link across the Tamar to Plymouth. Authorisation for the extension work was given in 1900 with the passing of the Bere Alston and Calstock Light Railway Act. So the complex manouvres and takeovers ended with the establishment of a new light railway between Plymouth and Callington.

The man entrusted with the work of changing the old narrow gauge line to standard and building the extension was a gentleman who never seems to stay for long out of the light railway picture: Colonel Stephens. This was to be his greatest engineering triumph, for the new line involved the building of a tremendous viaduct across the river. Seen from a distance, it looks like a handsome twelve-arch stone viaduct. Only when you get close up do you discover that it is not, in fact, stone at all but concrete, and lovers of statistics might care to know that it is 1,000ft long, 117ft high and a grand total of 11,148 blocks were used in its construction. An unusual feature in its early days was the waggon lift which could be used to move waggons between the railway and the quayside. That has long gone, but the viaduct remains and, what is more, remains in use. The line has been truncated, but passenger trains still run out of Plymouth up as far as Gunnislake.

The Tamar valley is an industrial archaeologist's paradise, and the railway is well represented in among the ruins of the once prosperous mines. Close to the crumbling engine house of Calstock Consols Mine you can still see the engine shed and water tower at the top of the incline that took the old mineral railway down to Calstock. There are reminders too of the river trade, that once worked with the railway, at Cotehele, round a bend of the river from Calstock, where one of the old trading barges has been restored. Much of the line can still be traced beyond Gunnislake to the original terminus at Callington under the shadow of Kit Hill, topped by an old mine chimney, placed there as a monument to Cornish miners. Best of all, of course, one can soak up the atmosphere of the Tamar valley by travelling the railway itself, which still retains all the quirky characteristics of a light railway.

Having tempted the reader with the resoundingly entitled Cleobury Mortimer and Ditton Priors Light Railway, now is the time to say something more about it. It did not perhaps ever live up to the splendour of its name, but it is an excellent example of a light railway constructed under the provisions of the 1896 Act. It had no pretentions to be other than what it was, a line of limited ambition, but ambition satisfied. In this at least the CM & DPLR (and if there was ever a case for using initials rather than a full title then surely this is it) fared very much better than several lines of greater pretensions.

The main source of freight traffic was the Abdon Clee group of stone quarries near Ditton Priors. Here there was an extensive narrow gauge rail system with level sections and rope worked inclines, all presenting a very busy industrial scene. There was also a second quarry group, the Magpie Quarries, which used an aerial ropeway. It was the need to get the stone to the main line route that brought the light railway into being, but if the origins were industrial the line itself was completely rural. An indication of the type of area through which it passed can perhaps be gained from one claimant's demand for compensation at the

time of building: £50 for the loss of rabbits. It was intended that the rural community should benefit as much from the new line as would the quarry owners, but the quarries were soon generating so much traffic that the passenger service had to be cut right back. The two 0-6-0ST Manning Wardles did sterling work and were frequently seen panting along with as many as twenty stone waggons in tow. It may have been a disappointment to would-be passengers who found services getting less and less frequent, but it was all very satisfactory to the board of directors.

Throughout its years as an independent railway, the CM & DPLR could fairly be described as a success. Then, in 1922, that independence was ended and the line that had enjoyed all the pride of its separate existence was suddenly no more than an insignificant branch of the Great Western Railway. What had on 31 December 1921 been a station was now on 1 January 1922 a mere halt. Goods traffic continued to thrive, though there was a falling off in passenger traffic as the motor coach began to take trade. Passenger services were ended but there was a new feeling in the air, though the feeling was not to be harnessed to railway action for many years. It was expected by the officials that the passenger service would end peacefully and quietly but, to their astonishment, hordes of railway enthusiasts appeared to celebrate the last rites. So many turned up to photograph and travel the line for the last time that aged coaches had to be pressed back into service. There is something rather touching about that last journey that seemed to take one back far beyond the year of 1938. The old coaches were still gas lit but before the end of the journey, the gas ran out. The train arrived at Cleobury Mortimer in suitably funereal darkness.

Goods traffic too was on the wane, but the coming of war gave a new importance to the line with the establishment close by of the Royal Naval Armaments Depot. The end was postponed, but not indefinitely. Closure arrived in 1965 with no great excitement; after all, the enthusiasts had already said their farewells twenty-seven years before.

CM & DPR had its origins in a known and well established group of quarries, but the East Kent Railway came into being almost by accident. It started because of a railway proposal, but one with far higher – or should one say lower – ambitions than the construction of a light railway. At the end of the nineteenth century, the South Eastern Railway and the London Chatham and Dover Railway agreed to share the cost for trial borings to test the ground for a railway tunnel beneath the English Channel. Well, as we all know, nothing much came of that in terms of transport at the time, but if railways beneath the sea were still many years away, the test borings did make a difference to the future of south-east England. They hit coal, and the Kent coalfield development began. Coalfields and railways have been intimately connected since the days of the earliest lines and soon plans were in hand for a line to link the collieries to the port of Richborough. The railway was part of the Stephens group and there were promises of great things as the coalfield developed and grew in importance. Sadly for all concerned, the coalfield's importance diminished rather than grew and with its decline the railway declined as well. It is a fact of life for all mainly industrial lines that their fate must inevitably be tied to that of the industry they serve. Even the enterprising Colonel Stephens could never manage to make this one a success.

Many industrial railway stories followed a similar route and it would be tedious to repeat them all. But the need for new routes to serve industry continued for as long as new industries needed bulk carriage by rail. Clay Cross in Derbyshire was a busy area of coal mines and iron works; Ashover stood on the edge of the Derbyshire Peak District and was liberally supplied with good, commercially valuable, limestone. Clay Cross could boast extensive rail connections; Ashover none. There was nothing therefore very surprising in the notion that the two should be linked by rail. What makes the Ashover Light Railway especially significant is that the date of its construction for the Light Railway Order was not obtained until 1922. It was to be a 2ft gauge line, the last important narrow gauge railway to be built in Britain and the consulting engineer for the project was none other than the ubiquitous Colonel Stephens. It was not to rank amongst his greatest achievements and passenger traffic seldom reached very considerable proportions. In fact, numbers travelling in the second year of operation were only half those of the first. Presumably the curiosity factor had led many to try the new line. Not that this would necessarily have bothered the owners, for they had never wanted to carry passengers in the first place and only did so because the government insisted on it as a condition of granting the Light Railway Order.

Thanks to the government's demand, the Ashover Light Railway not only carried passengers but did so in a bizarre collection of coaches. The first set delivered by the Gloucester Railway Carriage and Waggon Company Limited were more like tramcars than conventional railway coaches. Wooden seats ran longitudinally along each side of the coach and there were even leather loops in the roof for strap hangers. The next arrivals were very strange indeed and the name painted on the side 'Neverstop Railway' scarcely seemed appropriate for a line with thirteen halts in 7¼ miles. To add to the confusion, the wheels were rubber-tyred and flangeless, the coaches open to the elements with no protection at all on one side other than a safety chain and waist high wooden panelling on the other. They were, in fact, leftovers from the Great Wembley Exhibition of 1924 and 1925 when they formed part of a true no-stop train run on the Adkins-Lewis Rapid Transport System. On arrival at the Ashover Light Railway they were given rather more conventional wheels and put into service for summer excursions. To the relief of passengers, they were not used in winter.

Many find these old lines with their mixture of freight and passenger traffic to be among the most attractive of all light railways. In imagination, one can still see the busy sidings where the prosperous part of the railway trade was to be found in carrying the raw materials of industry. One can imagine too the long delays as trains were rearranged in a flurry of shuntings. Life on such a railway can never have been dull. The Ashover, like its compatriots, worked and prospered only for as long as the quarry prospered. But it was a line which could be relied upon to leaven the serious business of serving industry with the frivolity of excursions into the fine Derbyshire countryside. It is the mixture that helps to make such a line so appealing.

The Glyn Valley Tramway was opened in April 1873, from the wharf in Chirk on the Shropshire Union Canal, via exchange sidings at Chirk Great Western station to Glyn-Ceiriog, where the tramway connected with a granite quarry. The tramway was later extended in 1888, from Glyn-Ceiriog to Pandy, to connect with quarries in that area. The line was constructed to the unusual gauge of 2ft 4½ins and was operated by a fleet of three Beyer Peacock constructed 0-4-2 tram locomotives. The tramway later acquired a regauged, ex-L R O D Baldwin 4-6-0 tank in 1921, from the war disposals board. Here we see 0-4-2 tram locomotive *Glyn*, while shunting open wagons near Glyn-Ceiriog, c 1930. (*T. Middlemass Collection*)

0-4-2 tram locomotive *Dennis* hauls a train of four-wheeler carriages along the roadside section of the tramway, c 1910. The carriage stock was painted in green and white, with an attractive yellow key corner pattern lining, as can be seen here. The carriage stock consisted of four-wheeled closed and open vehicles, with oil lighting, as can be seen in this picture. The tramway closed to passenger traffic on 6 April 1933 and closed to all traffic on 6 July 1935. (*T. Middlemass Collection*)

The Baldwin ex-War Department 4-6-0 tank Glyn Valley Tramway number 4 stands with its crew in this picture, c 1925. This locomotive was obtained from the war disposals board in 1921 and regauged for use on the Glyn Valley Tramway. It was cut up after the line's closure in 1935. (*H. C. Casserley*)

2ft gauge, Dinorwic quarry slate wagons, being loaded on to the 4ft gauge transporter wagons at LLanberis on the Padarn Railway. The Padarn railway was opened in 1824, as a horse worked, 2ft gauge railway to transport slate from the Dinorwic quarries, later regauged and realigned to 4ft gauge in 1848. The Padarn Railway operated with steam traction from 1848, using two long wheelbase 0-4-0 tender locomotives, designed by Thomas Russell Crampton, named *Jenny Lind* and *Fire Queen*, constructed by A. Horlick of Northfleet in 1848. There was only one tender constructed, so only one locomotive ran at any given time. *Fire Queen* is preserved at Penrhyn Castle Museum and is on public display, along with Lord Penrhyns private carriage. The line later had three Hunslet constructed 0-6-0 tank locomotives, which were delivered between 1882 and 1895, to replace the original locomotives. (*Photographer Unknown*)

THE FINEST COACH TOUR IN WALES.

Cader Idris and Tal-y-llyn Lake.

Time Table for JULY, AUGUST & SEPTEMBER, 1907.

		a.m.	a.m.	p.m.	p.m.	p.m.	p.m.
Aberllefenny .. dep.	..	7m 5	10 0	12 20	1 55	4 45	..
Garneddwen .. ,,	..	a	a	a	a	a	..
Corris .. arr.	..	7m13	10 8	12 28	2 3	4 53	..

				a.m.			
TALYLLYN LAKE by Coach .. dep.	..	..	..	11 20	1 0	3 50	5 0
Corris ,, .. arr.	..	..	..	12 20	2 0	4 50	6 10

	a.m.	a.m.	a m.	p.m.	p.m.	p.m.	p.m.
Corris .. dep.	5m35	7 15	10 10	12 30	2 5	5 0	6 20
Esgairgeiliog .. ,,	a	7 22	a	12 37	2 12	5 7	6 27
Llwyngwern .. ,,	a	7 29	a	12 44	2 19	5 14	6 34
Ffridd Gate (for Llanwrin).. ,,	a	a	a	a	a	a	a
Machynlleth .. arr.	6 15	7 40	10 35	12 55	2 30	5 25	6 45

	a.m.	a.m.	a.m.	p.m.	p.m.	p.m.	p.m.
Machynlleth .. dep.	6 25	9 5	11 15	1 15	2 55	5 40	7 20
Ffridd Gate (for Llanwrin) .. ,,	a	a	..	a	a	a	a
Llwyngwern .. ,,	6 37	9 17	11 27	1 27	3 7	5 52	7 32
Esgairgeiliog .. ,,	6 43	9 23	11 33	1 33	3 13	5 58	7 38
Corris (for Cader Idris and Talyllyn Lake) arr.	6 50	9 30	11 40	1 40	3 20	6 5	7 45

		a.m.	a.m.	p.m.	p.m.	p.m.	p.m.
Corris by Coach .. dep.	..	9 35	11 45	1 45	3 25	..	..
TALYLLYN LAKE .. arr.	..	10 20	12 30	2 30	4 10	..	..

Corris .. dep.	6m52	9 32	11 42	1 42	3 22	..	7 47
Garneddwen .. ,,	a	a	a	a	a	..	a
Aberllefenny .. arr.	7m 0	9 40	11 50	1 50	3 30	..	7 55

a *Stops if required, passengers to inform guard.* m *Mondays only.*

Delightful Day or Half-Day Rail and Coach Outing.—From June 1st Conveyances will run at times as above between CORRIS and TALYLLYN LAKE, landing Passengers close to the foot of the Minfford Ascent, and allowing ample time for ascending CADER IDRIS. Fares—(By Coach), Single Journey, 1s.

Cheap Day Return Tickets are issued to Talyllyn Lake, Corris and Aberllefenny, from Aberystwyth, Borth, Aberdovey, Towyn, Barmouth, Dolgelley, Criccieth, Pwllheli, etc.

Cheap Day Return Tickets are issued to Talyllyn Lake from Whitchurch, Ellesmere, Oswestry, Llanymynech, Welshpool, Montgomery, Newtown, Llanidloes, Moat Lane, &c.

The Company give notice that they do not undertake that the Talyllyn Coaches shall start or arrive at the times specified in the Time Table, nor will they be responsible for any loss or inconvenience which may arise from delay, detention or injury of any nature. A limited number of Passengers only can be conveyed by each Coach and those having Through Rail and Coach Tickets will get precedence; those holding such 1st Class Tickets getting also preference to the Box Seats.

Timetable for the Corris Railway for July to September 1907. (*Author's Collection*)

Machynlleth, Corris Railway station, c 1910, with one of the Hughes, Falcon constructed 0-4-2st locomotives, on a train of two bogie saloon carriages and the four-wheeled brake van. This was the second station at Machynlleth, opened in 1907 to improve facilities for the growing amount of tourist and passenger traffic. (*Author's Collection*)

The River Dovey timber trestle bridge, c 1905. This was later replaced by a masonry and steel structure in 1907, which remained in use until 20 August 1948, when the line closed to all traffic. The train, with a Hughes, Falcon 0-4-2st and rake of new bogie saloon carriages, has been positioned on the bridge for this official picture. (*Author's Collection*)

Corris station, with its overall roof and combined carriage shed in the mid-1920s, just before the closure of the passenger services by the Great Western in January 1931. The Corris Railway had been owned from the 1870s by the Bristol Tramways and Carriage Company, who operated both the railway and, later, the local bus services. However as part of rationalisation by the Bristol Tramways, both the railway and its bus interests were handed over to the Great Western in 1930, who very quickly ceased to run passenger trains and soon sold the bus services to the Western Transport Company. (*Author's Collection*)

Towyn Wharf station, Talyllyn Railway, c 1930, showing the station and yard full of slate wagons awaiting unloading into standard gauge wagons. The reference to Wharf Station was in the context of a slate wharf, not that of a harbour, as in a transhipment from 2ft 3in gauge to standard gauge. (*Author's Collection*)

Talyllyn Railway locomotive number 1, *Talyllyn*, at Abergynolwyn station, c 1930, with a train of Brown Marshall four-wheeler carriages and the booking office brake van. Both the locomotives were constructed in 1865 by Fletcher Jennings of Whitehaven and survived on the line until preservation in 1951. The station building is a rather basic timber shelter, with a track layout consisting of a run around loop, which leads on to a mineral railway extension to Bryneglwys Quarry. (*Photographer Unknown*)

Opening day on the Plymouth Devonport & South Western Junction Railway, 2 March 1908, with crowds of people on the platform at Calstock station awaiting the first train. The P D & S W Jc Rly had running rights into Plymouth, operating a branch from Bere Alston on the main line to Plymouth, to Callington. The line originally had mineral traffic from the local arsenic mines, which were still in abundance in the first decade of the twentieth century. The P D & S W Jc Rly was one of the lines promoted by Colonel Stephens and had features similar to other lines constructed by the colonel, such as the station buildings, which were not unlike the corrugated iron buildings on the K & E S R. (*Author's Collection*)

Calstock station, c 1910, facing Bere Alston, with the viaduct in the background, with a train approaching from the far distance, bound for Callington. This picture shows the wagon lift on the viaduct, which connected the sidings and the quay on the River Dart, with the P D & S W Jr R. (*Author's Collection*)

An ex-L S W R 02 0-4-4 tank and train of three bogie carriages, cross the Calstock viaduct with a train for Bere Alston, from Callington. This is a good picture of the wagon lift, showing the girder supports of the approach line to the lift and the complicated arrangement for the lift itself. The line below connected local arsenic mines with the branch, here seen on 14 June 1926. (*H. C. Casserley*)

One of the Hawthorn constructed 0-6-2 tank locomotives, *Lord St Levan*, delivered in 1907 for mixed traffic work on the line. The three Hawthorn constructed locomotives, two 0-6-2 tanks and the single 0-6-0 tank became Southern Railway stock in 1923 and lasted in traffic to become British Railway's stock at nationalisation in 1948, not being withdrawn until the 1950s. (*Author's Collection*)

Liskeard & Caradon Railway. Hopkins Gilkes constructed 0-6-0st *Cheesewring*, at Moorswater, shunting stone wagons at the local quarry, c 1901. The L & C R was opened to traffic in 1844, using horse operation from the Moorswater Canal basin to Caradon mines. The line was extended in 1846 to Cheesewring and thereafter further extensions were made to Gonamena in 1859, to Tokenbury in 1860 and Kilmar, through the purchase of the Kilmar Railway in 1850. The line from Moorswater to Looe was opened on 27 December 1860 for freight, and 11 September 1879 for passenger traffic. The company took delivery of its first steam locomotive in 1862 and eventually had a fleet of three Hopkins Gilkes 0-6-0st machines by 1869. (*L C G B Ken Nunn Collection*)

0-6-0st *Cheesewring* at Moorswater locomotive shed, c 1901, showing the substantial stone buildings and the coal and watering facilities. The L & C R later acquired two more locomotives, a Robert Stephenson 0-6-0st, *Looe*, constructed in 1901, and an attractive 2-4-0 tank, *Lady Margaret,* constructed by Andrew Barclay in 1907. The railway was taken over by the Great Western on 1 January 1909 and is still part of the national network today, providing an important transport link with the main line in south Cornwall and the coast. (*L C G B Ken Nunn Collection*)

BRENDON HILL INCLINE.

The West Somerset Mineral Railway was opened in September 1859 and ran from Gupworthy to Watchet Harbour. The railway was owned by the Ebbw Vale Steel Company, who mined iron ore from the Brendon Hills and shipped it to South Wales via Watchet Harbour. The railway started to lose money in the 1880s when the deposits of good iron ore started to run out, and it was decided to close the line in 1898. A syndicate attempted to reopen the railway in 1907. However, although the new company acquired an ex-Metropolitan 4-4-0 tank and some rolling stock, the project came to nothing. A last use for part of the line came in 1909, when the Angus Company of New Zealand tested a new train braking system on the railway, using an ex-Great Western Dean 2-4-0 tender locomotive. The track was eventually lifted as part of the war scrap drive during the Great War. The picture depicts a train of the original company, with a Sharp Stuart 0-6-0st and four-wheeler carriages, at the foot of the Brendon incline, c 1885. (*H. H. Hole*)

A train full of false hope, with ex-Metropolitan 4-4-0 tank number 37 on an inaugural train up the derelict W S M R, on 4 July 1907. This project, which filled so many local people with hope, came to nothing and the line fell back into a derelict sleep, until lifted during the Great War. (*Local Post Card*)

A 1922 timetable poster for the Cleobury Mortimer & Ditton Priors Light Railway. (*Author's Collection*)

Cleobury Mortimer & Ditton Priors Light Railway.

Taken over by Great Western Rly – June 1922

TIME TABLE

NOVEMBER 2nd, 1921, and until further notice

WEEK DAYS ONLY.—MIXED TRAINS.

TUESDAYS AND THURSDAYS EXCEPTED.

UP.				A	B	C
				A.M.	P.M.	P.M.
DITTON PRIORS	...	dep.		11 0	12 30	3 50
Cleobury North Crossing		pass		D	D	
BURWARTON	...	dep.		11 15	12 45	4 0
Aston Botterell Siding	...	pass		—	—	
STOTTESDON	...	dep.		11 30	1 0	4 10
Prescott Siding	...	pass		—	—	
Detton Ford Siding	...			D	D	
Chilton Siding	...			—	—	
CLEOBURY TOWN	...	arr.		12 5	1 29	4 45
" "	...	dep.		12 6	1 30	
CLEOBURY MORTIMER JUNC.		arr.		12 20	1 45	

DOWN.				A	B	C
				A.M.	A.M.	P.M.
CLEOBURY MORTIMER JUNC.		dep.		9 18	10 55	2 30
CLEOBURY TOWN	...	arr.		9 28	11 5	2 40
" "	...	dep.		9 30	11 7	2 45
Chilton Siding	...	pass		D	D	D
Detton Ford Siding	...			D	D	
Prescott Siding	...			D		D
STOTTESDON	..	dep.		9 55	11 30	3 5
Aston Botterell Siding	...			D	D	
BURWARTON	...	dep.		10 13	11 45	3 20
Cleobury North Crossing	...	pass		D	D	
DITTON PRIORS	...	arr.		10 30	12 0	3 35

A Will run on Mondays, Wednesdays, and Saturdays only. Every exertion will be made for the 11.0 a.m. train from Ditton Priors to connect with the Great Western Company's train due to leave Cleobury Mortimer Junction at 12.38 p.m., but the Company cannot be responsible for any delay caused through late arrival.

B Will run on Fridays only.

C Will run on Wednesdays and Saturdays only.

D Calls if required.

Trains will not run on Christmas Day or Good Friday.

The Company do not guarantee that the trains shall start or arrive at the times printed, and liability cannot be accepted for any delay caused through late running of the trains.

E. J. MORRIS, General Manager

Cleobury Mortimer, October 20th, 1921.

H. G. Perkins, Printer, Load Street, Bewdley.

A 1922 timetable poster for the Cleobury Mortimer & Ditton Priors Light Railway. (*Author's Collection*)

Manning Wardle constructed 0-6-0st *Cleobury*, coupled to a brake van, c 1910. The Cleobury Mortimer & Ditton Priors Light Railway had two attractive Manning Wardle saddle tanks, both constructed in 1908, named *Cleobury* and *Mortimer*, which later became Great Western numbers 28 and 29. The C M & D P Lt Rly was opened on 1 July 1908 and ran from a junction at Cleobury Mortimer to Ditton Priors, serving the Abdon Clee quarries there. The company operated freight and passenger services on the line, in addition to mineral traffic. Later, after the Great Western took over the railway in 1923, the line had military stores traffic, from a Royal Naval Ordinance Depot. The railway lost its passenger service on 24 September 1938 and was then a freight only line. The R N O D, took over running military trains in 1956, using its own diesel shunting locomotives, until 1966 when the line closed completely. (*Author's Collection*)

A rebuilt number 28, *Cleobury*, on a mixed train leaving one of the wayside stations, c 1935, in the final years of the passenger service. The two Manning Wardle 0-6-0st locomotives were rebuilt at Swindon, by the Great Western in the 1920s, lasting in traffic until the 1950s. The original fleet of four ex-North London Railway four wheeled carriages were replaced with standard Great Western, Dean four-wheeled stock after the grouping in 1923. (*Lens of Sutton*)

The Ashover Light Railway was opened on 7 April 1925 and was constructed to 60cm gauge, using ex-L R O D, First World War field railway equipment. The railway ran from Clay Cross in Derbyshire to Ashover, over a 7 mile route, serving quarries and a pipe works owned by the Clay Cross Company. The railway was one of the light railways promoted and constructed by Colonel Stephens, who worked with the Clay Cross company on the project. The railway owned a fleet of ex-L R O D, Baldwin 4-6-0 tank locomotives and also used ex-War Department bogie open wagons for stone traffic. Here we see a Baldwin 4-6-0 tank, heading a train of one of the four bogie carriages, constructed new for the opening of the line by Gloucester Carriage & Wagon Company in 1925. The locomotives were named after the children of General Jackson – the chairman of the owning company – *Peggy*, *Guy*, *Hummy*, *Joan* and *Bridget*. There were two Baldwin locomotives, named *Guy*. The first *Guy* was meant to be renamed *Georgie*, but never carried the name plates. (*Ivor Gotheridge Collection*)

Roll over Baldwin, *Bridget*, after a derailment with a stone train, c 1930. This was a common problem with these American constructed machines, which had caused problems on the Western Front as well as on the Ashover Light Railway. (*Ivor Gotheridge Collection*)

Baldwin 4-6-0 tank locomotive, *Joan*, at Fallgate Yard, c 1935, surrounded by personalities of the line, including Harold Skinner, left, and Bill Banner, right. In the cab. P. C. Starling, right, and Mr Skinner Seniour, standing far left. (*Ivor Gotheridge Collection*)

Chapter Seven

Across The Sea To Ireland

Light railway development in Ireland was so different from that in the rest of Britain that it really does need a separate chapter – though some might argue that a separate book could scarcely do justice to the complexities of the Irish system. Ireland presented a very different situation for railway construction from that which was found in mainland Britain. Once the main trunk routes linking major towns had been established, there was little incentive to branch out into the thinly populated countryside, where there was little to offer in the way of goods traffic other than agricultural produce. Yet it was clearly desirable, if the country was to be developed, that railways should be brought to the regions, and it was agreed that some form of narrow gauge system might provide the answer. At the very beginning of the railway age in Ireland there had been much discussion about the gauge to be adopted. Arguments were finally resolved by a Gauge Commission, which set the standard at 5ft 3in. This decision was at last reached after careful deliberation. When it came to considering the provision of narrow gauge, the decision seems to have been almost entirely arbitrary. The gauge decided on was 3ft, which looks suspiciously like one of those compromise decisions, reached in the hope of satisfying everybody and ending up pleasing no one. Construction of such lines invariably meant a break of gauge wherever a standard gauge was met, but the disadvantages

of this should have been outweighed by the cheap construction costs of the narrow line. But a 3ft gauge is far too wide to be able to save much money for the builders. It was not a happy decision, and more problems developed out of the system adopted for financing these new routes.

The financial proposals probably derived from the English habit of regarding lreland as one of her colonies which required special treatment: the method that was very similar to one used in India – with equally disastrous results. The Irish Tramways Act of 1883 made the local authorities responsible for providing a guaranteed return to the investors. One can see how the argument ran. There is little in rural Ireland to encourage the entrepreneur so, unless we give a guaranteed profit, no one will invest. Who should pay the guarantee? Why, justice demands that the cash should come from those who benefit from the railway – the local people who will be served by it. Now this was very fine for the investor, but it gave him very little incentive to take an interest in the running of the line. All he had to do was collect the dividends. The local authority, however, was in a very different position. They could be saddled with the task of paying out money without being given any real say in how, where, or even whether the line was built. The Act, apart from providing an unsatisfactory system of railway finance, was even less satisfactory in other ways. The only supervisionary requirement was a clause that laid down that the Lord Lieutenant could order an inspection if he felt like doing so. As it appears that he frequently did not feel like doing so, one or two railways got away with murder – almost literally in some cases. The accident rate on lines such as the Tralee and Dingle Railway was at a level that would never have been tolerated elsewhere.

There were numerous Acts over the years, all intended to improve the provision of light railways in Ireland, culminating in the Light Railways (Ireland) Act of 1896, the Irish version of the important Light Railways Act of the mainland. It did little, however, to generate either fresh enthusiasm or fresh investment. Over the years too many lines had been built at excessive cost, too many of which had been badly planned and as badly managed. If ever there was a country that would have benefited from a sensibly worked light railway system, then Ireland was that country. Sadly, it got a system that was not particularly sensible and was seldom sensibly worked. In the twentieth century, the railways suffered as the whole country suffered from the enormities of civil war, and the division between the Irish Republic and Northern Ireland compounded the problem. It seems in many ways to be a sorry story, yet at the same time there was often a certain grandeur about the Irish lines. Many were built to main line standards in the provision of track and stations and though this usually added to their cost and contributed to their eventual decline, it gave them a fine air. If, for many of us, all Irish railways are forever populated by the shadowy figures of Will Hay, Graham Moffatt and Moore Marriott, then this does no more than show our ignorance, for

there were successes to be chalked up against the failures and there were lines that were well run and profitable. There were also, it has to be said, some disasters on a truly majestic scale.

The original impetus to light railway builders came with the need to extend the somewhat skeletal main line routes to reach a wider area. A popular area for developers was the south-west of Ireland, in particular the region around Cork. Ireland's first railway, opened in 1834, had linked the city of Dublin to the port of Kingstown, now Dun Laoghaire, and proved a great success. Cork sat at the edge of an estuary that formed a fine natural harbour. Queenstown, later to be known as Cobh, was then an attractive fishing town, but was to develop, like Dun Laoghaire, into a busy international port. Between the two was a narrow passage on the west bank of which sat, not unreasonably, Passage West, usually known simply as Passage. Here was a situation that could be developed along the lines of the Dublin to Kingstown Railway, and the promoters hoped for a similar success. Plans were put forward for a railway link between Cork and Passage, which was intended to link in with an existing steamer service. Approval was received but early enthusiasm was not matched by early finance and another eight years drifted by until Parliament approved the Cork, Black Rock and Passage Railway.

On 15 June 1847 Lady Deane delicately removed a sod of earth with a silver shovel, placed it in a decorative wheelbarrow and trundled it away for a few yards. Bands played, guns fired, crowds cheered and healths were drunk. Work had officially begun and a large number of men with less ornate shovels and undecorated barrows began their labours. Almost exactly three years later the railway was opened to the public – and how the public adored it. Six thousand people crowded into the trains that first weekend. Everything seemed well set for a profitable venture and, indeed, the railway was a success. But it was a success that depended in large measure on the steamer services with which it was linked, and this was to prove a major problem for many years to come. The directors of the railway formed their own company to provide a steamer service between Passage and Queenstown, but this aroused fierce opposition from the older steamship companies and led to a bitter price-cutting war. The row between the 'railway steamers' and the rest rumbled on for years, and it often seemed that as fast as the railways made money, the steamers lost it.

One answer to the recurring problem eventually emerged – reduce the steamship travel distance by increasing the distance travelled by railway. An extension to Crosshaven was proposed, but it was quickly realised that a broad gauge line would be an unnecessary expense, so a 3ft gauge line was recommended. There was, however, clearly very little sense in building an extension to a line in a different gauge from that of the original, so it was decided to re-lay the whole of the original track as narrow gauge. The Act was passed in 1896 and work began on expanding the old railway and re-establishing it as a light railway. All railway history is liberally spattered with optimistic estimates of construction costs that prove not merely a little optimistic but wildly inaccurate. Here was yet another. The physical difficulties proved far greater than the engineers had anticipated, especially on the ground near Passage where an underground spring was encountered, which no amount of pumping and damming seemed able to stem.

Then a common economic blight fell on the works: the money ran out. Yet in spite of all these problems, work was finally completed, just four years behind schedule. In June 1904 the whole of the new railway was open, offering as the official handouts had it, 'the cheapest and most expeditious route through the unrivalled scenery of the River Lee'.

The railway was a success, but again the somewhat expensive paddle steamers proved a drain on the company. Where the steamer route duplicated the rail route, few used the former, not wanting the bother of changing from one means of transport to the other, so that the Monkstown–Crosshaven steamers were often empty. Excursions were a quite different matter, and combined rail and river trips proved extremely popular. Those who know the region – and probably even those who do not – can readily imagine the attraction of taking the little train down to the waiting steamer. Steam by rail and steam by water is certainly an appealing mixture in this age, which is singularly short of both commodities.

The line might quite well have gone on quite nicely but for the effects of war, starting with the Great War of 1914–18, which brought new demands and new working practices to all British railways. Irish railways were, however, soon to feel the disastrous effects of a war fought much closer to hand – the Civil War. Cork was, for a time, a Republican stronghold, and to prevent the approaching troops using the railway the Carrigaline Bridge and the Douglas Viaduct were both destroyed in August 1922. For eight months no trains ran and it was not until the end of 1923 that things really began to get back to normal. All this was more than the somewhat wobbly finances of the little company could stand. It was taken over by the Great

Southern Railway, but the 'great' was no longer to apply to the Cork, Blackrock and Passage Railway, and it began to slide towards oblivion. It closed in 1932.

The railway had been successful enough in a way, and was immensely popular, a great favourite with day-trippers and excursionists. Its conversion to a light railway had breathed new life into the old enterprise, but always the steamers had proved more expensive to run than had been expected and had brought in less income than had been hoped. Looking at the nature of the line it is difficult not to think that things could have been, or should have been, better. But whatever the hopes for the line, war had shattered the dreams. And what war had begun was completed, as elsewhere, by the motor bus, which ate into the tourist trade. Other railways suffered a similar fate, even when they began offering a destination that was, if anything, even more popular than the steamer pier.

Our next line, also built out from Cork, was typical of the light railways built under the local authority guarantee system of the 1883 Tramways and Public Companies (Ireland) Act. It was the Cork and Muskerry Light Railway, more popularly known as the 'Blarney Tram'. One of its main purposes was to get in on the popular tourist traffic to Blarney Castle, where those who were prepared to hang out over the battlements could kiss the Blarney Stone. One has a splendid image of a train load of reticent passengers setting out from Cork, eyeing each other warily from behind their newspapers in the style approved on English railways – to be followed by a return journey when everyone talked at once, and golden phrase after golden phrase tripped from every tongue. Those who knew the Blarney Tram in the old days do not,

alas, support the fantasy. Everyone, it seemed, talked as much going out as they did coming back, for the passengers were mainly local Irish, and the average Cork man has never been in need of any extra powers to set him talking.

This was a scheme which had everything one could want to see in a light railway project. There was a steady two-way traffic, with coal and supplies going out from the city to the country and agricultural produce coming from country to town. This is the bread and butter of all lines: Blarney Castle provided the jam. So it is somewhat surprising to find the whole enterprise getting off to a very shaky start. The line looked very sensible: a main route from Cork to Coachford with a branch to Blarney, but under the new system of Baronial (local authority) guarantees, the company had to leap several official hurdles before they even reached the starting line. Proposals had to be submitted to the Grand Jury, the Irish equivalent of a County Council, from where it was passed to the Privy Council and, even after that, a bill still had to be passed through Parliament. It is scarcely surprising that many railway schemes proposed under the legislation never even started construction.

The Cork and Muskerry Light Railway Company was incorporated in December 1883 and set off for the first of its obstacles. Just what a wearisome process this could be can be gauged by looking at the time spent between then and the passing of the Act in June 1886. One can only sympathise with the would-be railway builders who spent two and a half years enmeshed in paper work. Once that stage was complete, however, they came into their own. Contracts were speedily handed out, work was begun and on 2 July 1887 the Board of Trade inspector was able to view the completed line and declare it 'the best eight and a half miles of permanent way he had seen on any tramway'.

In character the line was a mixture of conventional light railway and steam tramway. Much of it ran along the verge of the road, but it was worked with conventional narrow gauge engines, the first a 2-4-0 tank locomotive from the Falcon Works in Loughborough, and conventional light railway coaches and waggons. The method of working the trains was not, however, all that it might have been. In some respects, the safety measures employed on the railway were exemplary, with an efficient signalling system and block working using colour coded staffs. The line was divided into seven blocks, and before a train could be cleared to proceed it had to have a 'line clear' ticket, which could only be obtained by the insertion of a correctly coloured staff. This all had to be done by the guard, and was one of his more important duties. It was a lot safer for him personally than some of his other tasks. The guard also had to collect tickets from the passengers and in order to do so he had to swing from carriage to carriage. It was no easy matter to move across while the sleepers rattled beneath your feet and the carriages swayed and jerked to an irregular rhythm; a single slip would mean the guard was down on the track with death as the only prospect. Sadly, this was to prove the fate of more than one guard on the Blarney Tram.

A.T. Newham's history of the line contains a long account of experiences in the 1920s by Rev John Scanlon who was to become the Auxiliary Bishop of Honolulu. It is mainly concerned with the troubles, when the passengers were as likely to be injured by the IRA attacking soldiers on the train as by the Black and Tans stopping the train to take hostages for their own safe passage. But there is mention here, too, of another

source of revenue for the line, and rich revenue at that for a hydro had been established at St Ann's, or St Annes or St Anne's depending on whose spelling you fancy. There the wealthier citizens went for cures for whatever they were convinced ailed them – and when they travelled they travelled first class. No doubt in response to the demands of this trade the local station was soon dignified with a ladies waiting room. So the line enjoyed many years of prosperity, years that proved so prosperous, in fact, that an extension was soon put in hand, a branch to Donoughmore that almost doubled the length of the railway.

There is no need to detail the subsequent history of the line, whose steady decline followed the construction of urban tramways in the Cork area and the later arrival of the motor bus. It passed to the Great Southern Railway and there was a brief burst of activity at the time of the Cork Exhibition of 1932. It was a false dawn, for the railway was not to survive to the end of the year. But if its fate was the fate of so many small concerns, it went down with pride undiminished for unlike so many others it had for a time at least paid its way. It had failed through no fault of planning nor through inefficiency of operation, but simply because the times had changed and events had overtaken the Blarney Tram.

Having moved on from light railway to light railway come tramway, we can now take one further step and look at an out and out steam tramway. This ran from Terenure on the south side of Dublin, where it joined the Dublin United Tramways system, to the town of Blessington, 15½ miles away in the foothills of the Wicklow mountains. It was built to the 5ft 3in gauge and was later extended to Poulaphouca. There was little, at first glance, to distinguish it from many another similar route. The prospectus made the usual hopeful noises about the traffic that could be expected from 'several mills and manufactories along the line' and promised that only 'the newest and most improved engines, carriages and trucks' would be used. The first engine was, in fact, a Falcon 0-4-0WT of the typical, enclosed tramway type, with machinery and moving parts tucked decorously away behind iron skirts. The rolling stock was, in a sense, very typical tramway stock as well – but typical of the horsedrawn urban tramway not the steam powered rural tramway. The coaches had two decks and the sides were open to the elements. In theory this was splendid news for the passengers, for the line climbed steeply out of Dublin to reach a point of 700ft above sea level with magnificent views right across to the mountains of Mourne. In practice, the view often consisted of little more than black smoke blowing in through the open carriages. The locomotives had tall chimneys designed to carry away the smoke but these were not unduly effective and the trains presented a bizarre appearance, with the high stack locomotives wheezing up the steep gradient hauling tramcars that looked like refugees, making an escape bid from the city streets.

The line was neither more nor less profitable than many another of its type, just as it was neither more nor less prompt in its timekeeping than its confreres. It was, however, somewhat less reliable than was altogether desirable, and more experienced passengers were known to sling bicycles on the back of the tram to ensure at least some form of transport for the journey. It was notoriously accident prone. The first death occurred in the first year, though it was not generally held

to be the railway's fault. The victim was born a little simple and had already managed to walk into the path of a moving cart which had made her simpler still. There were to be many fatalities in the history of the tramway which were attributable less to the inborn simplicity of the victims as to the stupidity brought on by the demon drink. Mourning relations of the deceased usually put crosses by the line to mark the fatal spot, and so many appeared along the way that the Dublin and Blessington Tramway came to be known as the world's largest graveyard.

The tramway, as with all such tramways, fulfilled for a time a role that was later to be taken by road transport, and is notable now mainly for its strange looking mixture of locomotives and tramcars. But it is nowhere near as strange as our last example of the Irish light railway. It provides an interesting question for a railway quiz. Question: where in Britain could you have found an 0-3-0 locomotive? Answer: the Listowel and Ballybunion Railway. Those who do not know the line and are desperately trying to envisage a sort of steaming tricycle will now be put out of their misery. No one seems to know quite how, or more especially why, the builders of the line linking these two towns discarded earlier plans for a conventional narrow gauge railway and opted instead for what was known as a monorail system, but was in reality a three-rail elevated transport system. It is known, however, that after the usual arguements had been to-ing and fro-ing between opponents and supporters of a rail link, the promoters were approached by Charles Francois Marie-Therese Lartigue who was, it is perhaps unnecessary to add, French. He was full of enthusiasm for the system which he had patented all over Europe and North and

South America, which sounded very impressive. No doubt he was rather more reticent about the number of lines that had actually been built: a steam line in France and a mule worked one in Algeria. The system consisted of a monorail mounted on A-frames. Locomotives and rolling stock were built so that they overhung on either side of the line, ensuring a low centre of gravity, and stability was provided by two further tracks set on either side and below the monorail. All kinds of claims were made for the system: it would be cheap to build, would take up less land than a conventional railway and would be cheap to run. The Irish were convinced and work began in 1887.

The central rail was 3ft 3in from the ground and was very light by railway standards, only 27lb per yard. The first locomotives were in effect double, rather like the well-known Fairlies except that here the two units sat on either side of the track instead of being put back to back and the driver perched in the middle. Elaborate arrangements had to be made for road crossings, for no ordinary level crossing would do. The simplest crossings were made by using a hinged section of rail which could be swung to one side and, when opened, automatically set a semaphore signal on the line. Elsewhere drawbridges were constructed across the track. Conventional points could not be used so sections of track were curved so that they could be swung round, the ends describing a circle, with loop lines and sidings meeting at the perimeter.

Perhaps the most remarkable thing of all about the Lartigue system was that it worked, and indeed worked quite remarkably well. It became a tourist attraction for the district, for there was nothing like it to be found anywhere else in the British Isles. In the early years of this century it even managed to show a profit, which was more than could be said of many a conventional railway. It did suffer from several inherent problems, particularly with the moving of freight. Stability could only be achieved if the trucks could be balanced on either side of the track. This was no problem if you wished to move, say, a load of coal. You simply distributed it evenly. It was more of a difficulty, however, if you wished to shift one grand piano. One thing all were agreed upon was that the Listowel and Ballybunion Railway was great fun.

The Irish light railway story is not full of huge successes, largely in the first place because the narrow gauge lines were built too wide and were thus too expensive. The guarantee system did little to help promoters as there was often considerable opposition from ratepayers who could see the very real possibility that they could be left to pay the bills. Then there was the uniquely Irish element: the civil war and subsequent partition of the country. But when the end came for many of these lines, it came for much the same reason as it had in England, Scotland and Wales. The new door-to-door service of private car and lorry took away the railway trade. Throughout Britain small railways passed into history. But that is not quite the end of the story.

The Cork Blackrock & Passage Railway was opened on 8 June 1850, as a 5ft 3in gauge line, from Cork to Passage. The railway was converted to 3ft gauge in 1900, double tracked and extended to Crosshaven in 1904. The original company had operated a fleet of three 5ft 3in gauge, Sharp Brothers 2-2-2 WT locomotives, which were replaced with four Neilson constructed 2-4-2 tank locomotives, after conversion to 3ft gauge. The line also replaced its elderly Irish standard gauge four-wheeler carriages, with handsome narrow gauge bogie carriage stock in 1900. Here we see a 2-4-2 tank on a train of bogie carriage stock, about to depart the Cork terminus for Crosshaven, c 1928, after the takeover by the Great Southern Railways in 1925. (*Author's Collection*)

Three of the four Cork Blackrock & Passage 2-4-2 tanks, headed by number 6 P, at Cork shed, on 10 June 1932, after the closure of the line beyond Monkstown on 1 June 1932. The locomotives are painted in G S R unlined green in this picture, and illustrate the railway in its last years before closure to all traffic, which took place on 19 September 1932. The line was dismantled shortly after closure, with the carriage stock being scrapped, however some of the wagons and locomotives found a new lease of life on the Cavan & Leitrim Railway, where they worked until its closure on 1 February 1961. (*H. C. Casserley*)

The Cork & Muskerry Railway was opened to traffic on 8 August 1887, from Cork to Blarney, further extensions being opened to Donoughmore on 6 May 1893 and to Coachford on 18 March 1888. The line was 3ft gauge, and served the agricultural area west of Cork, also catering for the then growing tourist trade. The railway prospered for a short time, until the post-Great War period, when revenues started to decrease, as a result of road competition. In 1925 the railway was taken over by the Great Southern Railway, who eventually decided to close the line, as it was a considerable loss maker, this taking place on 31 December 1934. 4-4-0 tank number 4 Blarney, heads a train into Cork city on 10 June 1932, sharing its route with the Cork City electric tram system.

The other 3ft gauge narrow gauge system in south-west Ireland was the Schull & Skibbereen, which ran from Skibbereen to Schull, a route that hugged the coast and was popular with tourists when the line opened on 6 September 1886. The line became part of the Great Southern Railways in 1925 and, like many other Irish rural lines, was a loss maker; this being reflected in its closure, which took place on 15 April 1944. In the case of the S & S Lt Rly, as a result of the Second World War and its effect on the economy of the Irish Free State, it was temporarily reopened on 10 December 1945 and closed finally in 1946. 4-4-0 tank number 4 heads a mixed train along a roadside section of the S & S Lt Rly, c 1936. (*C. Cockell*)

The Dublin & Blassington Steam Tramway opened to traffic on 1 August 1888, operating from Terenure to Blassington at first and then being extended to Poulaphouca in 1895, with a further extension to Terenure in 1896. Electrification was looked at in 1911, however the Great War intervened and this proposal was never taken any further. The extension line to Poulaphouca was closed in 1927 and as a result of road competition, the rest of the tramway closed to all traffic on 31 December 1932. The tramway was constructed to 5ft 3in gauge and was operated using 0-4-0st tram engines. Here we see a Manning Wardle example, without its tram skirts and sporting a long stove pipe chimney, hauling a train of two double deck, bogie tram cars, c 1920. (*L C G B Ken Nunn Collection*)

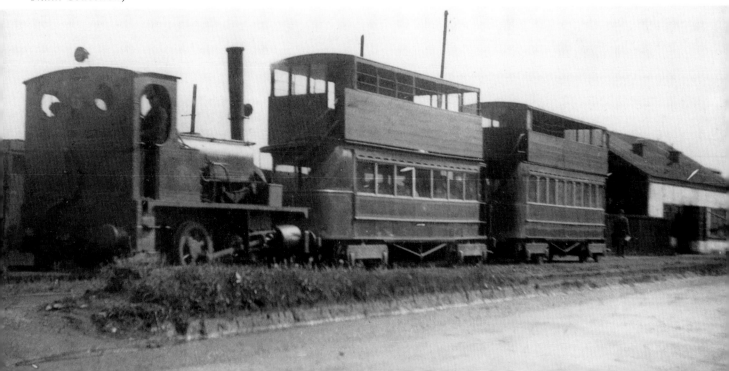

There were few monorails in Britain, however probably one of the most famous and best-loved example existed in southern Ireland, that of the Listowel & Ballybunion, which was opened on 1 March 1888 and connected both the towns. The company had a strange lineage, in that it was an English registered company, operated in Ireland, using a French system of monorail, constructed by a German engineer – truly international. The system had been tested in London, on a circle of track at Tothill Fields near the Houses of Parliament, before the Irish line was constructed. The monorail was not a total success and like most monorails had its share of problems, which included transhipment of goods and distribution of weight on each side of the train, involving some strange remedies. The line suffered during the Irish Civil War, in the early 1920s, when it was sabotaged on a number of occasions. Finally, as a result of the Civil War and a lack of interest by the Great Southern Railway, in absorbing the line, it closed in 1924 and was dismantled soon after. One of the two Hunslet constructed 0-3-0 tender tank locomotives used on the line waits with a train at Ballybunion station. There was also an upright boilered machine, ex-Tothill Fields experimental railway, which was used to construct the line in 1888. Locomotive No 2 is seen here on 31 May 1924, shortly before closure. (*Author's Collection*)

One of the Hunslet 0-3-0 locomotives nears Liselton Station, the only intermediate stop on the Listowel & Ballybunion Railway, c 1920. This picture depicts a typical train formation with two carriages, one of the staircase waggons, essential for crossing the line at stations and a string of waggons. (*L C G B Ken Nunn Collection*)

The other way to cross the line, by the drawbridge, as shown in this picture. (*L C G B Ken Nunn Collection*)

An early picture of the Listowel & Ballybunion, showing Hunslet 0-3-0 locomotive number 1, with its large headlight, posed for an official photograph at Listowel. This picture shows the track layout to good effect, with the station and goods shed in view. Also one can see the turntable used as a point for accessing the main line and sidings, c 1890. (*Author's Collection*)

1891 constructed Hunslet 2-6-0 tank *Argadeen*, was probably one of the most attractive light railway locomotives in Britain. The locomotive was one of two machines on the Timoleague & Courtmacsherry Extension Light Railway, in south-west Ireland. The 9 mile long light railway was constructed to 5ft 3in gauge and opened on 24 April 1891, operating between the two towns, partly as a road side tramway and partly as a conventional railway. The company was taken over by the Great Southern Railways in 1925 and by the C I E in 1945, passenger services being withdrawn in 1947. The line had a daily freight service and special excursion trains until 1960, when C I E, withdrew all services from the line. The other locomotives were also Hunslet products, an 0-6-0ST of 1885 named *Slaney* and an 0-4-2ST of 1890 named *St Molaga*. The locomotives were identified by their names, rather than numbers, and were painted in a plain black livery. (*L C G B Ken Nunn Collection*)

Tralee & Dingle Railway, Hunslet 2-6-0 tank number 3 heads a mixed train at Tralee station, c 1928. The T & D R was opened on 31 March 1891, linking Tralee with Dingle 32 miles away, on the west coast of Ireland. The railway also had a branch from Castlegregory Junction to Castlegregory, on Tralee bay, which was 6 miles in length. The railway operated a fleet of seven 2-6-0 tank locomotives and a solitary Hunslet 2-6-2 tank, now preserved, all constructed by Hunslet and Kerr Stuart. The railway also had an 1889 constructed Hunslet, double-cabbed tram type 0-4-2 tank locomotive, number 4, which was scrapped in 1908. The company had a fleet of twenty-one, first and third class bogie carriages and a modern fleet of wagons, both bogie and four-wheeled vehicles. The T & D R was taken over by the Great Southern Railways in 1925, losing its passenger service on 17 April 1939 and was again taken over by C I E in 1945. The line finally closed to freight and cattle traffic in June 1953, a weekly cattle train being the last traffic on the line, in conjunction with the local cattle market. The remaining locomotives and some of the freight stock was then transferred to the Cavan & Leitrim Railway, for further use. (*Author's Collection*)

On 29 June 1954, Hunslet Bn 3 class 4-6-0 tank 7c shunts wagons in Ennis yard, while making up a freight. This 1922 constructed locomotive was once named *Malbay*, being part of an eleven strong fleet of motive power supplied by three different locomotive manufacturers. The line was in fact two separate railways, The West Clare Railway, opened on 2 July 1887, from Ennis to Miltown Malbay, and the South Clare Railway, opened on 3 August 1892, from Miltown Malbay to Kilkee and Kilrush via Moyasta Junction. The whole line covered a distance of 48 miles from Ennis to Kilkee and 47 miles to Kilrush, operating freight and passenger services when first opened. The line became part of the Great Southern railways in 1925 and was taken over by C I E in 1945, closing to all traffic in 1961, despite an attempt to save money by using new Walker Diesel railcars and diesel mechanical locomotives in the late 1950s. (*F. A. Wycherley*)

The Cavan & Leitrim Railway was one of Southern Irelands best-loved narrow gauge lines, opened on 17 October 1887, from Belturbet Junction, on the Great Northern main line connecting to the Great Northern Railway line to Dromod, on the Sligo line – a distance of 33 miles. A branch to Arigna was opened on 2 May 1888, which tapped the traffic from the local coal mines, which added a further 15 miles. The picture shows one of the Robert Stephenson 4-4-0 tank locomotives number 8, *Queen Victoria*, with a train of balcony end bogie carriages, waiting to depart Belturbet station in 1920. The railway had a fleet of eight Robert Stephenson 4-4-0 tanks and one solitary Robert Stephenson constructed 0-6-4 tank, named *King Edward*. The carriage stock consisted of twenty-two balcony end, bogie vehicles, and the freight stock was made up of a large fleet of four-wheeled vans, cattle vans and open wagons. The line was taken into the Great Southern Railways group in 1925 and taken over by C I E in 1945, then closed to all traffic on 1 February 1961. (*L C G B Ken Nunn Collection*)

Ballinamore Station, with its passing loop and extensive goods yard, c 1950. Note the large number of freight vehicles, mostly cattle vans and open wagons in the distant sidings. It was at this location that the old company established its locomotive, carriage and wagon repair works. The works functioned until the late 1930s, when it was decided to send any locomotives needing heavy repairs to Inchicore, Dublin. The carriage and wagon repair shops continued until the line closed in February 1961, even rebodying a carriage as late as 1958. (*Author's Collection*)

The unsuccessful Robert Stephenson H N 1 class 0-6-4 tank, *King Edward*, C & L R Number 9. This locomotive, constructed in 1904, was not liked by footplate crews and was not a welcome addition to the motive power on the C & L R. Number 9 was overweight and of a very clumsy design, being seldom used in traffic and finally succumbing to the cutter's torch in 1934. (*Author's Collection*)

During the inter-war period, half of the fleet of original 4-4-0 tank locomotives on the C & L R were withdrawn and scrapped. In order to replace the missing locomotives, the Great Southern Railways and later C I E, supplied machines from other narrow gauge lines. Here we see former Tralee & Dingle 2-6-0 tank number 6T, being turned by its crew. The line acquired a mixture of former T & D R, 2-6-0 tanks and the solitary 2-6-2 tank, now preserved, which on the C & L R, were known as Kerrymen. Also the line was backed up, with the complete stud of former Cork, Blackrock and Passage Tank Locomotives, with their ungainly lanky 2-4-2 wheel arrangement. The freight wagon fleet also benefited from the demise of other narrow gauge lines, having a selection of wagons from the C B P R, T & D R and the W C R. (*J. W. P. Rowledge*)

The Dundalk Newry and Greenore Railway was a subsidiary of the London & North Western Railway, which straddled the border between Northern and Southern Ireland. The project to construct and develop the D N & G R was conceived in the 1860s by the L N W R, in order to exploit the considerable traffic in cattle, farm produce and tourism then existing between Ireland and the rest of Britain. The 26 mile long line constructed to 5ft 3in gauge, was opened from Greenore to Dundalk in 1873 and extended to Newry in 1876. A harbour was developed at Greenore, for ferry traffic to Holyhead, with a frequent steam ferry service between the two. The L N W R also developed a golf course and hotel for the growing Victorian tourist traffic, at Greenore, which was very popular until the outbreak of the Great War in 1914. At the grouping in 1923, the D N & G R, became part of the London Midland & Scottish Railway, who operated it directly until 1933, when operations were transferred to the Great Northern Railway of Ireland. On 1 January 1948, the line became part of the British Transport Commission, who decided to close the line on 31 December 1951. The company, which operated in Northern Ireland and the Republic, took six years to wind up, not being wound up until 1957. Here we see a long mixed train headed by one of the three L N W R Crewe constructed 0-6-0 ST locomotives, leaving Dundalk for Greenore, c 1925. (Author's Collection)

The Fintona horse tram waiting at Fintona Junction station, c 1955, with Dick the horse about to set off for Fintona Town. The Fintona tramway existed as a result of the construction of the Great Northern Railway of Ireland main line from Omagh to Enniskillen, which bypassed Fintona. In order to serve Fintona, a mile-long branch was constructed and worked as a tramway, using horse power for the passenger service. A daily freight train ran using a steam locomotive, which usually ran in the early morning before passenger trams started. Regardless of gender the horse was always called Dick and the locals referred to the horse tram as the van. The horse tram lasted until the closure of the main line, with the last working on 30 September 1957, after which all the railway network in the area closed for good. The tram car was more fortunate in that it can still be seen in the Ulster Folk and Transport Museum at Cultra, near Belfast. (*J. W. P. Rowledge*)

The Clougher Valley Railway was a 3ft gauge rural tramway that connected with two Great Northern Railway of Ireland main lines and ran from Maguire's Bridge to Tynan. The line was opened on 2 May 1887, using steam power on passenger and freight trains along its 36 mile formation. The company later obtained internal combustion motive power, which it used in conjunction with its steam fleet. Here we see the Walker rail car number 1, at Fivemile Town station on 15 June 1937, in the last years of the railway. The Clougher Valley Railway closed to all traffic on 31 December 1941. (*Mile Post 92½ Picture Library*)

The Giant's Causeway Tramway was opened in June 1882, connecting Portstewart to the Giant's Causeway, a distance of 7 miles. The line originally had steam motive power, but was later converted to Electric traction on 5 November 1883, however some steam traction continued in use until 1899. Here we see one of the tram locomotives on a train of four-wheeled cars at Giant's Causeway, c 1880. (*Author's Collection*)

A picture from a later period at Giant's Causeway station, on 10 August 1930, with two of the electric trams and trailers in the yard. Note the pagoda like corrugated iron shelter in the middle distance. The tramway finally closed to traffic in 1949, however there is a restored section of the line which, in recent times, has reopened. (*H. C. Casserley*)

The 3ft gauge Portstewart Tramway was opened in June 1882, connecting Portstewart station with the town, a distance of just over a mile. The line had three Kitson 0-4-0 tram locomotives and operated a fleet of two bogie double-deck tramcars and an open four-wheel car. The tramway was taken over in 1897 by the Belfast & Northern Counties Railway, which in turn became a part of the Midland Railway Northern Counties Committee. In 1923 the line became a part of the L M S as the L M S, N C C, being closed completely in 1926 and was soon dismantled. However, two of the attractive Kitson tram locomotives were preserved; number 1 at Hull Transport Museum and number 2 in the Ulster Folk and Transport Museum at Cultra near Belfast. One of the Kitson tram locomotives waits with a bogie open top tram car and luggage van at Portstewart station, c 1920. (*L C G B Ken Nunn Collection*)

Three foot gauge Ballymena & Larne 2-4-2 tank number 103, stands at a wayside station with a van train, c 1930. There were three of these Bayer Peacock constructed machines, dating from 1908. This example was withdrawn by the L M S, N C C in 1938, while the other two lasted until the lines closure under the Ulster Transport Authority in 1950. The B & L R opened to traffic on 1 August 1877, becoming part of the Belfast & Northern Counties Railway in 1889, which in turn was acquired by the Midland Railway in 1903. It was finally grouped in 1923 into the L M S, N C C. The line operated an extensive passenger and freight service, including boat trains from Larne harbour to Ballymena. As part of the Ulster Transport Authority, the line was closed during the rationalisation of branch lines in 1950. (*Author's Collection*)

The County Donegal Railway was one of Ireland's most famous 3ft gauge lines. Here we see a passenger train at Stranorlar, headed by Nasmyth Wilson constructed 4-6-4 tank number 14 *Erne*. This locomotive was one of two machines of this type out shopped in 1904, remaining in service until the lines closure on 31 December 1959. The C D R was one of the most extensive narrow gauge lines in Ireland, with branches to Londonderry, Latterkenny, Killybegs, Glentiies and Ballyshannon. The railway was jointly owned by the Great Northern Railway of Ireland and the L M S, N C C, which managed the line through a committee. (*Photographer Unknown*)

Walker rail car number 10 stands at Stranorlar station, c 1955, attached to the ex-Dublin & Blessington trailer, number 16. The C D R had a sizable fleet of railcars, including products constructed by Walkers of Wigan and even a set purchased and re-gauged in 1926, from the standard gauge Derwent Valley Light Railway in Yorkshire. A number of these sets are preserved in several collections in Northern Ireland and on the Isle of Man, where the two newest Walker rail car sets operated after sale from the C D R. (*Photographer Unknown*)

Neilson constructed 4-6-0 tank number 8, *Foyle*, shunts wagons at Stranorlar, c 1928. The County Donegal Railway had a fleet of interesting locomotives over the years, from small 2-4-0 tanks to large 2-6-4 and 4-6-4 machines. The railway had originally been constructed to 5ft 3in gauge, being converted to 3ft gauge in 1894. At the time of closure in December 1959, rolling stock had been standardised to the large tank locomotives and rail car operation. After the railway operations ceased, the company went over to operating buses and a road delivery service for some years, before the company was amalgamated with C I E and the U T A. (*Author's Collection*)

The Londonderry & Lough Swilly Railway was first opened as a 5ft 3in gauge line, on 12 November 1863. However, by 1885, the railway had constructed extensions from Londonderry to Latterkenny and Buncrana. The L & L S Rly was converted to 3ft gauge in 1883, with extensions to Carndonagh and the construction of the Burtonport Extension by the early 1900s. Here we see Hudswell Clarke constructed 4-8-4 tank number 6, on a long train of nine bogie carriages, c 1925. The Latterkenny & Burtonport Extension was constructed using a government grant and had its own locomotives and rolling stock, which were not meant to be used on the main L & L S R. Like many other Irish narrow gauge lines described in this book, the L & L S R suffered from road competition and closed its rail services in stages from the late 1940s, until the last section of line finally closed to freight traffic from Londonderry to Buncrana in August 1950. The company continued as a bus and road haulage operator until 2013, when it finally went into liquidation and ceased operation. (*Author's Collection*)

Beyer Peacock 2-4-0 tank number 4, *Loch*, constructed in 1874, stands at the head of its train at Douglas station on the Isle of Man Railway, c 1950. The Isle of Man Railway was opened from Douglas to Peel on 1 July 1873, the line to Port Erin following on 1 August 1874. The Manx Northern Railway, which ran to Ramsey, was opened on 29 September 1879 and was later amalgamated in to the I O M railway on 24 February 1904. A further railway extension took place in June 1887, with the opening of the Foxdale Railway, which was operated by the I O M railway. Like the passenger carrying narrow gauge railways in Ireland, the Isle of Man network was constructed to 3ft gauge. (*Author's Collection*)

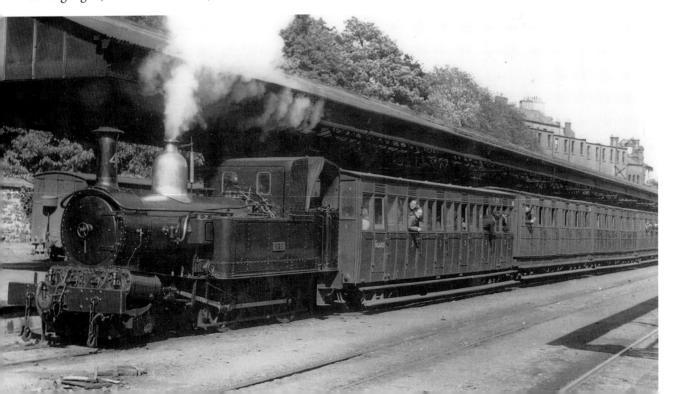

The most modern I O M railway Beyer Peacock 2-4-0 tank locomotive is number 16, *Mannin*, constructed in 1926, here seen in company with the only 0-6-0 tank locomotive on the line, ex-Manx Northern Railway number 15, *Caledonia*, constructed by Dubs in 1885, outside Douglas motive power depot, c 1930. (*Author's Collection*)

The Groudle Glen Railway was opened to traffic in 1895, being constructed to 2ft gauge in order to connect Groudle, on the Manx Electric Railway, with the sea lion and polar bear enclosure at Sea Lion Rocks on the coast. The railway had two small W. G. Bagnall 2-4-0 tank locomotives, both now preserved, *Polar Bear* constructed in 1908 and *Sea Lion* constructed in 1898, which operated from the early days until the original company's closure in 1962, apart from a brief period in the 1920s when battery locomotives were used. Here we see *Sea Lion*, in its original lined green livery, at the Sea Lion Rocks terminus, c 1896. (*Author's Collection*)

Polar Bear nears the terminus at Sea Lion Rocks in this picture, c 1949. Note the distinctive W. G. Bagnall four-wheel carriages in the train formation. (*Author's Collection*)

The overall roof terminus at Groudle on the Groudle Glen Railway, c 1925, with one of the short-lived troublesome 2-4-2 battery electric locomotives, *Sea Lion*. The steam locomotives soon returned to the line and were the mainstay of operations until the original company closed the railway in 1962. The railway was restored by volunteer enthusiasts from 1982-1986, who formed a preservation society, to run the line as a heritage operation. Today one can still take a trip behind *Sea Lion* along the coast to Sea Lion Rocks, while riding in a Bagnall four-wheeler carriage. (*Local Postcard*)

Chapter Eight

Railway Phoenix

Throughout this book, each line has had a history that followed a somewhat familiar pattern: an early period of prosperity, followed by decline and closure. There have been a few exceptions, such as the Vale of Rheidol and the Snowdon Mountain Railway, which have been kept going entirely on the strength of a well-established tourist trade. That might have been the end of the tale, but for a quite separate decision taken by British Rail that affected all railways – main line, branch line and light railways alike. That decision was to call an end to the age of steam, the dread blow finally falling in 1968. The end was in sight, however, long before that. On 18 March 1960, the last steam locomotive to be built for British Railways, a 2-10-0 Class 9 goods was named at Swindon Works as *Evening, Star*, a lovely and appropriate name, for night was indeed, it seemed, about to fall over the steam age of Britain. But though British Rail had declared that the age was over, there were thousands of enthusiasts who had a different point of view. They were in love with railways, and steam railways in particular. And long before that final blow could fall, events in the light railway world had already shown what might be done.

In the late 1940s, L.T.C. Rolt who had been staying at Talyllyn decided to take a ride on the Talyllyn Railway which was still, if only just, functioning. He arrived at Tywyn to find no staff, no simmering engine, nothing except a bland notice saying simply 'No Trains Today'. Unable to steam up the line, he walked it instead and in walking it fell in love with it. In October 1950 he called a meeting in Birmingham at which fellow enthusiasts joined him in considering ways in which the railway might be saved. The result of that meeting was the formation of the Talyllyn Preservation Society. The full story of the founding of the society and their splendid efforts to keep the line alive is told in Rolt's book *Railway Adventure*, and stirring stuff it is. Today, when railway preservation is an accepted part of the British scene, it is perhaps difficult to imagine how daunting the situation must have seemed to those pioneers. These amateurs had decided to take over and run a 7½ mile long railway of severe gradients with decrepit track, ancient locomotives and equally antique rolling stock. On any other railway, they would have had a chance to beg, borrow or obtain at moderate cost, some suitable rolling stock. But, to add to their problems, they were acquiring a line built to the unusual gauge of 2ft 3in. Only two other public railways had ever been built to such a gauge, the Campbeltown and Machrahanish line but that, alas, had long since gone out of business. There remained only a near neighbour, the old tramway line, the Corris Railway, which had gone first to the GWR and then into the ownership of British Rail. It was then being dismantled. The rails had gone for scrap, but two venerable locomotives were available and thanks to a decidedly helpful attitude on the part of officials at Swindon, the society was able to acquire them at a bargain price. One major problem had been solved, and very soon gangs of volunteers were busy on the line and in the workshops. The rebirth of the Talyllyn Railway had begun. It was no simple task but it was accomplished. Looking back on that epic story now, more than thirty years after the event, it seems almost a miracle that those enthusiastic amateurs did succeed. But for the fact that no one in Whitehall seemed to know that the railway still existed as a going concern at all, it would already have followed many other light railways into the nationalisation bag. It would then doubtless have been sold off piecemeal and would have disappeared from view. As it was, the amateurs were able to take over an existing, viable company and simply – though there seemed little simple about it at the time – carry on working. The Talyllyn prospered and prospers, a light railway that has lost its original function as a mineral line serving the slate quarries but has survived to bring delight to all lovers of steam. It remains one of the most attractive railways in Britain and its success has been an inspiration to others.

Rolt at the end of his book had this to say of the line he and his colleagues had worked so hard to save: 'The Talyllyn Railway is not simply an engineering museum piece; it is a local institution and as such it has become a part of Wales and Welsh life … we have striven against odds not merely to preserve a railway but to keep alive a spark of that fine tradition which flourished so richly when the Talyllyn line was born. Is it not worth cherishing?' The question was rhetorical, but we can now look back over the years and confirm what Rolt half believed, half hoped. The Talyllyn adventure was worth while, not only for its own sake but because it was to prove an inspiration to others. Other narrow gauge railway preservation schemes followed, notably the famous Festiniog Railway. Then in 1960 the first standard gauge line was taken over – the Middleton Colliery Railway, the first railway in the world to be regularly worked by steam locomotives. There could hardly have been a more appropriate candidate for the part of first preserved standard gauge line.

The preservation movement gathered strength and is still growing. Narrow gauge and standard gauge, main line and branch line, industrial railway and passenger railway – all have been tackled by the enthusiasts. Some run over no more than a mile or so of track, while others are major commercial operations attracting a great tourist trade. Among the success stories are many lines which started out as light railways, the old Kent and East Sussex which ran at the heart of the Colonel Stephens empire being an outstanding example. There are also railways which began as industrial lines and have undergone a very light railwayish transformation to emerge as passenger carrying routes. It is worth looking at one or two of these in more detail, for they provide interesting examples of ways in which seemingly lost causes can, with a little imagination, be turned to successes.

Let us take as a first example the Sittingbourne and Kelmsley Light Railway, built primarily to serve the Bowater paper mills. Why should anyone want to keep it once its usefulness as a freight carrier had ended? Is it merely that given a length of track anywhere you can always find some idiot to run a steam engine along it? Some might argue that case but it would not, in my view, be true of the Sittingbourne and Kelmsley. It is precisely the industrial origins of the line that gives it its special appeal. You plunge into that world right at the start, as the line snakes away around tight curves over the end of a creek which is crossed on embankment and viaduct. Down below the water swirls and bubbles, stained by industrial waste. An assortment of pipes, some dull, some shining silver in the sun, twist round over and below the line so that you might believe you were in a space station – if you were not chugging sedately behind a tank engine that had just celebrated its fiftieth birthday. The line is a reminder of the role the light railways once played in the industrial life of the country. It is narrow gauge, as is the Leighton Buzzard Railway which began life by supplying sand to industry to replace supplies from Belgium which became unavailable during the Second World War. The Leighton Buzzard line may lack the splendid site enjoyed by the Kentish line, but compensates for that in being able to show a rich variety of narrow gauge locomotives. The Foxfield Light Railway, on the other hand, takes us right back to the origins of the whole railway system as the servant of collieries, in this case in Staffordshire. It is the type of line which, but for its new role as a passenger carrier, would never have featured in this list at all.

These lines show how industrial routes can find a new use, and they also show how a successful adaptation need not mean a loss of character. They were lines that were not necessarily built as light railways but have, as it were, achieved light railway status. The same can be said of other preserved lines which have lost their roles as part of a national rail system but have reopened as steam railways. Whatever status they may have had in the past, these lines must now be run in accordance with a Light Railway Order. Those who drafted the Light

Railway Act did so because they believed it was the only way in which railways would be brought to all the communities who needed railways. They could hardly have imagined that the same idea could be used to provide railways run less for profit than for pure fun and pleasure. But is there so very much difference between the two notions after all? In both cases the legislation has simply been used to enable people who want railways to get railways.

The later years have not been altogether devoid of new plans and new activities. In 1960 work began on a brand new line, the Lincolnshire Coast Light Railway, a genuine original route in the tradition of the older seaside lines. True, a good deal of the initial impetus came from enthusiasts who wanted somewhere to run narrow gauge locomotives, but the line itself was thought of as one that would appeal to holiday makers. Its planning and running were in the best Stephens' tradition of simplicity and economy. However, like so many of its predecssors, it fell a victim to changing tastes and habits. But it was not merely abandoned: the whole enterprise with its fine collection of engines and rolling stock was moved to the Skegness Water Leisure Park, where trains are still run to delight visitors.

But there was also one outstanding example of a light railway which has no function in life other than to give pleasure – pleasure to those who travel on it and, more especially, to the man who owned and ran it. If you had walked across the churchyard at Cadeby in Leicestershire on a Saturday afternoon in summer then the chances are you would have found the rural peace suddenly broken by the shrill of a steam whistle. Look across the gravestones and from behind the handsome old rectory a locomotive would have emerged, the Rev E.R. Boston on the footplate. This was the Cadeby Light Railway, Teddy Boston's very own line. It is a curious fact that there seems always to have been a strong streak of railway enthusiasm among the clergy. I once asked Teddy Boston about this, and he quoted another railway cleric in reply: 'The steam railway is very like the Church of England – the best way of getting to a good place.' Teddy died in 1986, and if anyone ever deserved to end up in a good place, then he was that man. He and his little railway are sadly missed. Both John Scott-Morgan and I have many happy memories of riding the footplate with Teddy or bowling round the surrounding country lanes on his traction engine, beguilingly named *Fiery Elias*.

For many years the light railways offered the population of remote and peaceful corners of Britain a new and better way of reaching the town, the market, the sea or whatever other good place they hoped to reach. They served the community well and looking through the records of these old lines, it is clear that they aroused real local enthusiasm and affection. At one point it seemed that the light railways' day was done, but the enthusiasts have helped to bring some back to life. Stand on Tenterden Town station and perhaps as the train pulls in it will be drawn by a Hunslet tank engine, one of that very popular class of 0-6-0ST locomotives found on so many lines. But this one has a name: *Holman F. Stephens*. The clock seems suddenly to turn back and you half expect to hear a polite 'thank you, Sir' from the porter as he accepts a cigar from a tall gentleman of military bearing. The great age of light railways may have passed, but the spirit of the light railway age lives on.

The 2ft 3in gauge Campbeltown and Machrihanish Light Railway was Scotland's only independent, narrow gauge light railway. The line opened to mineral traffic in 1877 to Kilkevin colliery and was further extended to Drumlemble in 1881. The railway was finally opened to Machrihanish with a passenger service on 16 August 1906, thus allowing a rail connection across the peninsular from Campbeltown. Here we see one of the Andrew Barclay constructed 0-6-2 tank locomotives, either *Argyll* or *Atlantic*, awaiting departure from the terminus at Campbeltown, c 1925. (*T. Middlemass Collection*)

0-6-2 tank *Atlantic* simmers at the opposite end of the line, Machrihanish, on 2 August 1930. The railway had a fleet of handsome bogie balcony end carriages, which were painted dark olive green and ivory white, with black underframes and white roofs. The 0-6-2 tank locomotives were painted in a livery not unlike the North British Railway colour scheme of bronze green with black smokebox and cab roof and red buffer beams. The line also had three other locomotives, an Andrew Barclay 0-4-2 ST named *Chevalier*, a second Barclay 0-4-2 WT named *Pioneer* and a Kerr Stuart 0-4-2 Skylark class tank named *Princess*. These smaller tank locomotives were painted plain black. The railway started to lose money in the years after the Second World War and suffered from road competition, finally closing down in September 1931. (*H. C. Casserley*)

An information post card handed out to passengers on the line, c 1920s. (*Author's Collection*)

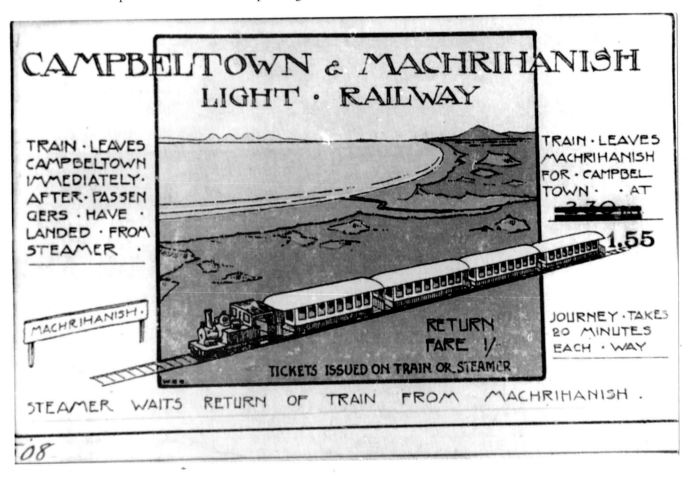

CAMPBELTOWN & MACHRIHANISH
LIGHT · RAILWAY

TRAIN · LEAVES CAMPBELTOWN IMMEDIATELY · AFTER · PASSENGERS · HAVE · LANDED · FROM STEAMER ·

MACHRIHANISH ·

TRAIN · LEAVES MACHRIHANISH FOR · CAMPBELTOWN · · AT

RETURN FARE 1/-

TICKETS ISSUED ON TRAIN OR STEAMER

JOURNEY · TAKES 20 MINUTES EACH · WAY

STEAMER WAITS RETURN OF TRAIN FROM MACHRIHANISH ·

08

At the Vale of Rheidol Light Railway Swindon, constructed 2-6-2 tank number 7 enters the station at Devil's Bridge, with a train from Aberystwyth, c 1995. In 1988 British Rail sold the Vale of Rheidol Light Railway to a private company, which has in the last quarter of a century invested a considerable amount of capital to improve the railway as a heritage and tourist line. (*Anthony Burton*)

Talyllyn Railway number 3, *Sir Haydon*, simmers in the platform at Abergynolwyn, with a train for Towyn, c 1996. The Talyllyn Railway was saved by a group of railway enthusiasts, led by Tom Rolt in 1951, becoming the words first heritage railway. Today the line is operated by volunteers and is an important part of the tourist industry in mid-Wales, along with six other narrow gauge lines. (*Anthony Burton*)

The locomotive sheds at Ravenglass with three of the 15in gauge miniature locomotives outside, c 1930. (*Author's collection*)

The Sand Hutton Railway was opened in 1912 on the estate of Sir Robert Walker. The line was originally constructed to 15in gauge, but was later re-gauged to 18in gauge in 1922, when the owner purchased a large quantity of ex-W. D. narrow gauge track materials and four Hunslet 0-4-0 Well tank locomotives. Here we see locomotive number 12 with a single bogie carriage and brake van at one of the wayside stations, c 1925. The railway had a public passenger service, from 1922 and was gradually extended, until the line reached Bossall and Barnby House, a distance of 4 miles. The railway also served the estate, including a branch to a brick works at Claxton, which provided traffic to the main line junction at Warthill, served by the L N E R. The railway proved to be uneconomic and was closed to all traffic in March 1932. (*Author's Collection*)

The Welshpool & Llanfair Light Railway opened on 4 April 1903 and connects Welshpool with Llanfair via Castle Caereinion. The 2ft 6in gauge line was constructed to transport agricultural produce from the local farms to Welshpool, where it was transhipped on to the main line. The railway was operated by the Cambrian Railways, until 1923, when it was taken over by the Great Western and was in turn taken over by British Railways after nationalisation in 1948. The railway closed to passengers on 9 February 1931 and was closed to freight on 3 November 1956, after which a preservation society was formed to save the line. Here we see Beyer Peacock 0-6-0 tank number 823, *Countess*, crossing the road in Welshpool, on its way to the main line station, c 1955. (*Author's Collection*)

A roadside scene on the W & L with Locomotive 823, *Countess*, heading a train of open wagons on its way to Llanfair, c 1947. (*Author's Collection*)

Towards the closure of the W & L line, there were a number of rail tours operated by railway societies. Here we see a photo stop on the tour organised by the Birmingham Locomotive Club in 1956, shortly before the end of freight services. (*T. Middlemass Collection*)

A scene taken in 1903, shortly after the opening of passenger services on the Welshpool & Llanfair Light Railway, with locomotive number 1, *The Earl*, later Great Western number 822, at Llanfair terminus, showing the locomotive crew, guard and entire station staff. (*T. Middlemass Collection*)

Principal Light Railways In Britain

The following list of principal light railways is arranged in chronological order by date of opening. Closure dates are given at the end of the entries. 'O' indicates that a line is still open. 'PO' indicates that the line is partially open.

Opened		Closed
1801	Penrhyn Railway	1962
1806	Swansea & Mumbles Tramway	1963
1823	Plymouth & Dartmoor Railway	1912
1824	Padarn Railway	PO
1825	Redruth & Chacewater Railway	1915
1829	Pentewan Railway	1970
1832	Saundersfoot Railway	1939
1836	Festiniog Railway	O
1844	Liskeard & Caradon Railway	PO
1850	Cork Blackrock & Passage Railway	1932
1856	Lee Moor Tramway	1960
1859	Corris Railway	PO
1859	West Somerset Mineral Railway	1909
1860	Croesor Tramway	1941
1863	County Donegal Railway	1959
1863	Londonderry & Lough Swilly Railway	1948
1865	Talyllyn Railway	O
1866	Bishop's Castle Railway	1935
1866	Shropshire & Montgomeryshire Railway	1960
1867	Mawddwy Railway	1951
1868	Festiniog & Blaenau Railway	1990
1869	Bury Port & Gwenraeth Valley Railway	1995
1870	Garstang & Knott End Railway	1963
1870	South Shields, Marsden & Whitburn Colliery Railway	1953
1872	East Cornwall Mineral Railway	1908
1873	Glyn Valley Tramway	1935
1873	Snailbeach District Railway	1950
1875	Ballymena Cushendall & Red Bay Railway	1940
1875	Ravenglass & Eskdale Railway	O

Opened		Closed
1875	Wantage Tramway	1946
1876	Culm Valley Railway	1979
1877	Ballymena & Larne Railway	1942
1877	Campbeltown & Machrahanish Light Railway	1931
1877	Rowrah & Kelton Railway	1926
1877	Welsh Highland Light Railway	1937
1879	Southwold Railway	1929
1880	Ballycastle Railway	1948
1880	Torrington & Marland Railway	1985
1882	Port Stewart Tramway	1926
1883	Giants Causeway Tramway	1949
1883	Wisbech & Upwell Tramway	1966
1884	Castlederg & Victoria Bridge Railway	1933
1885	Bestbrook & Newry Tramway	1948
1886	Schull & Skibbereen Light Railway	1944
1887	Cavan & Leitrim Railway	1957
1887	Clougher Valley Railway	1941
1887	Cork & Muskerry Railway	1932
1888	Dublin & Bressington Tramway	1932
1888	Listowel & Ballybunion Railway	1924
1891	Easingwold Light Railway	1956
1892	West Clere Railway	1960
1894	Lee on the Solent Light Railway	1935
1895	Eaton Hall Railway	1946
1895	Rye & Camber Tramway	1939
1895	Tralee & Dingle Railway	1955
1896	Pwllheli & Llanbedrog Tramway	1928
1896	Snowdon Mountain Railway	O
1897	Selsey Tramway	1935
1897	Weston Clevedon & Portishead Light Railway	1940
1898	Lambourn Valley Railway	1978
1898	Lynton & Barnstaple Railway	1935
1898	North Sunderland Light Railway	1951
1900	Kent & East Sussex Railway	PO
1901	Basingstoke & Alton Light Railway	1901
1901	Bideford Westward Ho & Appledore Railway	1917
1901	Corringham Railway	2013
1901	Leadhills & Wanlockhead Light Railway	1938
1901	Sheppey Light Railway	1950
1901	Wrington Vale Light Railway	1950
1902	Dornoch Light Railway	1960
1902	Vale of Rheidol Light Railway	O

Opened		Closed
1903	Axminster & Lyme Regis Light Railway	1966
1903	Welshpool & Llanfair Light Railway	PO
1903	Great Orme Tramway	O
1904	Kelvedon & Tollesbury Light Railway	1934
1904	Mid Suffolk Light Railway	1952
1904	Tanat Valley Light Railway	1964
1907	Nidd Valley Railway	1936
1908	Cleobury Mortimer St Ditton Priors Light Railway	1967
1908	Plymouth Devonport St South West Junction Railway	PO
1911	Red Lake Tramway	1933
1912	Derwent Valley Light Railway	1979
1912	East Kent Railway	PO
1912	Sand Hutton Railway	1932
1913	Ewden Valley Railway	1929
1915	Kingsnorth Railway	1940
1920	Edge Hill Light Railway	1925
1925	Ashover Light Railway	1950
1925	North Devon & Cornwall Junction Railway	1965
1925	Totton, Hythe & Fawley Light Railway	O
1925	Wissington Light Railway	1957
1927	Romney Hythe & Dymchurch Light Railway	O

Further Reading

Bonsor, N.R.P., *The Jersey Eastern Railway* (Oakwood)

—— *The Jersey Railway* (Oakwood)

Boyd, J.I.C., *The Festiniog Railway* (2 vols, Oakwood)

Cartwright, R. & Russell, R.T., *The Welshpool & Llanfair Light Railway* (David & Charles)

Catchpole, L.T., *The Lynton & Barnstaple Railway* (Oakwood)

Comfort, N., *The Mid-Suffolk Light Railway* (Oakwood)

Davies, D.L., *The Glyn Valley Tramway* (Oakwood)

Davies, W.J.K., *The Ravenglass & Eskdale Railway* (David & Charles)

Garrett, S.R., *The Kent & East Sussex Railway* (Oakwood)

Hall, R.M.S., *The Lee Moor Tramway* (Oakwood)

Heaviside, G.T., *Narrow Gauge Into the Eighties* (David & Charles)

Jones, K., *The Wotton Tramway* (Oakwood)

Kidner, R.W., *Minor Standard Gauge Railways* (Oakwood)

—— *The Romney, Hythe & Dymchurch Railway* (Oakwood)

Maggs, C., *The Weston Clevedon & Portishead Railway* (Oakwood)

Milner, W.J., *The Glyn Valley Tramway* (OPC)

Price, M.R.C., *The Lambourn Valley Railway* (Oakwood)

Prideaux, J.D.C., *English Narrow Gauge Railways* (David & Charles)

—— *Irish Narrow Gauge Railways* (David & Charles)

—— *Welsh Narrow Gauge Railways* (David & Charles)

Reading, S.J., *The Derwent Valley Light Railway* (Oakwood)

Rolt, L.T.C., *Railway Adventure* (David & Charles)

Scott-Morgan, J., *British Independent Light Railways* (David & Charles)

—— *The Colonel Stephens Railways* (David & Charles)

Turner, K., *The Leek & Manifold Valley Light Railway* (David & Charles)

Turner, K. & S., *The Shropshire & Montgomeryshire Light Railway* (David & Charles)

Turner, S., *The Padarn & Penrhyn Railway* (David & Charles)

Whitehouse, P.B., & Snell, J.B., *Narrow Gauge Railways of the British Isles* (David & Charles)

Woodcock, G., *Minor Railways of England and their Locomotives* (Goose)

Index